The Handbook of
NONSEXIST WRITING

The Handbook of NONSEXIST WRITING

Second Edition

Casey Miller and Kate Swift

PERENNIAL LIBRARY

HARPER & ROW, PUBLISHERS, New York
Cambridge, Philadelphia, San Francisco, Washington
London, Mexico City, São Paulo, Singapore, Sydney

To the memory of
T'Et and Aunt Kack

Permissions acknowledgments appear on page 181.

THE HANDBOOK OF NONSEXIST WRITING (*Second Edition*). Copyright © 1980, 1988 by Casey Miller and Kate Swift. All rights reserved. Printed in the United States of America. No part of this book may be used or reproduced in any manner whatsoever without written permission except in the case of brief quotations embodied in critical articles and reviews. For information address Harper & Row, Publishers, Inc., 10 East 53rd Street, New York, N.Y. 10022. Published simultaneously in Canada by Fitzhenry & Whiteside Limited, Toronto.

Library of Congress Cataloging-in-Publication Data

Miller, Casey.
    The handbook of nonsexist writing.

    Bibliography: p.
    Includes index.
    1. Rhetoric.   2. Sexism in language.
I. Swift, Kate.   II. Title.
PN218.M5   1988   428.2   87-45648
ISBN 0-06-181602-7   88 89 90 91 92   MPC   10 9 8 7 6 5 4 3 2 1
ISBN 0-06-096238-0 (pbk.) 88 89 90 91 92   MPC   10 9 8 7 6 5 4 3 2 1

Contents

Preface

For whatever reasons—goodwill, a sense of justice, an editor's instructions, the pursuit of clarity—a growing number of writers and speakers are trying to free their language from unconscious semantic bias. This book is intended for them. It will probably be of no use to people who, for an equal number of complex reasons, actively oppose linguistic change or fail to detect the messages of prejudice others hear.

Much of the unconscious bias embedded in modern English stems from cultural attitudes toward women and, to a lesser but significant extent, from cultural expectations damaging to men. Comparable considerations affect members of other groups, since standard usage also conceals biases based on race, religion, ethnicity, sexual preference, age, and physical handicaps. In focusing on the problems of linguistic sexism, we have tried to make our examples and discussion applicable by analogy to these other human conditions as well.

Many of our examples come from published sources or from radio and television. We used quotation marks to indicate these examples, and we kept the names of public figures when they occurred. If a quotation included the name of someone not widely known, we substituted conventional designations like John Doe and Jane Roe out of respect for the person's privacy. All examples not in quotation marks are made up, and personal names occurring in the latter, other than the names of public figures, are also made up and do not represent real people.

We can attest to the authenticity of all the examples we quoted, but because they are intended to be illustrative only, we did not include their sources. In addition to providing practical suggestions, our aim throughout has been to show why an apparently innocuous word or phrase may be injurious. Documentation for quotations of substance and for the academic studies cited is included in a section beginning on page 167.

We are grateful to several friends who read and criticized the manuscript—Virginia Barber, Nancy Henley, James and Ruth Oliver, and Nancy Wilson—and to many others who sent us material, especially Sanford Berman, Anne S. Bittker, K. D. Codish, Paula Kassell, Marie Shear, and Patricia Summers. Our editor, Carol Cohen, not only provided many ideas and examples, but it was she who recognized the need for a book of this kind in the first place and invited us to write it. Our debt to her is one we acknowledge with special appreciation and thanks.

Casey Miller and Kate Swift

Use is the judge, and law, and rule of speech.

—Horace, c. 12 B.C.

When established idiom clashes with grammar, correctness is on the side of the idiom. Put another way, if sticking grimly to rules of grammar makes you *sound* like a pompous pedant, you *are* a pompous pedant.

—William Safire, 1983

Introduction:

Change and Resistance to Change

When the first edition of *The Handbook of Nonsexist Writing* appeared in 1980, efforts to eliminate linguistic sexism had already gained support from a wide assortment of national and local organizations, both public and private. Guidelines for nonsexist usage had been issued by most major textbook publishers, and professional and academic groups ranging from the Society of Automotive Engineers to the American Psychological Association were developing their own guidelines, as were such diverse public institutions as the City of Honolulu and the University of New Hampshire. Churches and synagogues were struggling with the problems of perception raised by traditional male-oriented language; librarians were rethinking the wording of catalog entries; and groups as varied as philanthropic foundations, political councils, and consumer cooperatives were re-casting their charters, bylaws, application forms, and other materials in gender-neutral terms. Advertising copy had begun to acknowledge that bankers, insurance agents, scientists, consumers at every level, farmers, and athletes are female as well as male.

By the mid-eighties the movement toward nonsexist usage had gained so much momentum that researchers who studied its impact by analyzing three recently published American dictionaries of new words were prepared to state, in the cautious phraseology of scholarship, that their results showed "a trend toward nonsexism" in written language. The data, they said, "provided a judgment of the efficacy of feminists' efforts toward nonsexist vocabulary," and they ventured the opinion that the "importance and justice of the subject have been recognized."

During the same period, a marked increase occurred in academic research into language use and its relation to women, and the number of books and articles on the subject addressed to the general public continues to grow. So extensive is this outpouring, in fact, that a newsletter established in 1976 to report on activities in the field grew in only ten years from a 4-page pamphlet to a 64-page periodical called *Women and Language*. Not all this interest has been on the side of linguistic reform, of course; opposition to the concept of nonsexist language continues and in some quarters has stiffened. But during the past ten years, some of the most influential opponents of linguistic change have been persuaded that the problem is not going to disappear as obligingly as ground fog on an autumn morning.

The increased use of nonsexist language by those in major channels of communication provides a graphic demonstration of the mysterious ways in which reality affects language and is, in turn, affected by it. For as women become more prominent in fields from which they were once excluded, their presence triggers questions of linguistic equity that, once having been asked and answered, bring new visibility to women. How does one refer to a woman who is a member of Congress, or address a woman who sits on her country's highest court or is its chief of state? What does one call a woman who flies in space? Superficial as such questions may seem, their existence brings into focus a new awareness of women's potential. When *Time* magazine named Corazon Aquino its "Woman of the Year," it paid tribute to her extraordinary achievements and, at least by implication, made two other statements: (1) the year's most newsworthy person need not be a man, and (2) some of the connotations once assumed to be communicated only by the word *man* are now attaching themselves to the word *woman*. Still to come, however, is widespread acceptance of a gender-inclusive term that, in such a context, would concentrate attention on the person's newsworthiness rather than on the irrelevant factor of gender.

Notable among recent acknowledgments of the need for more even-handed usage was the change of policy adopted by the *New York Times* regarding titles of courtesy. First the *Times* stopped prefixing women's names with honorifics in both headlines and sports stories—thereby including women under the same rubric it had followed for years with respect to men. Then the newspaper dropped its ban on the courtesy title *Ms.* because, as an Editor's Note explained, "The Times now believes that 'Ms.' has become part of the language." Since the *Times* moves to a majestic beat, it is not about to rush headlong into the unqualified adoption of a nonsexist lexicon, but the recognition of *Ms.* wasn't its first move in that direction, and each day brings new evidence that it was not intended to be its last.

As individuals and the media gradually work out the logic involved in each new linguistic quandary, the presence of women in government and business and in the arts and professions becomes more and more apparent. Which is not to say that as women gain positive linguistic visibility they magically gain recognition and respect. But something "magical" does happen whenever people—singly or as a class—begin to sense their potential as fully integrated members of society, and it is this "magic" that using nonsexist language helps to bring about.

One subtle, and therefore particularly harmful, linguistic practice that has not changed much in the last few years is the use of common-gender terms as though they automatically refer only to males. When a member of Congress says on a televised news program, "Any politician would have trouble running against a woman," or a newspaper reports that a man "went berserk . . . and murdered his neighbor's wife," the effect is to make women irrelevant. Politicians become, once again, an all-male breed, and a woman, denied even the identity of "neighbor," is relegated instead to that of "neighbor's wife."

The reason the practice of assigning masculine gender to neutral terms is so enshrined in English is that every language reflects the prejudices of the society in which it evolved, and English evolved through most of its history in a male-centered, patriarchal society. We shouldn't be surprised, therefore, that its vocabulary and grammar reflect attitudes that exclude or demean women. But we are surprised, for until recently few people thought much about what English—or any other language for that matter—was saying on a subliminal level. Now that we have begun to look, some startling things have become obvious. What standard English usage says about males, for example, is that they are the species. What it says about females is that they are a subspecies. From these two assertions flow a thousand other enhancing and degrading messages, all encoded in the language we in the English-speaking countries begin to learn almost as soon as we are born.

Many people would like to do something about these inherited linguistic biases, but getting rid of them involves more than exposing them and suggesting alternatives. It requires change, and linguistic change is no easier to accept than any other kind. It may even be harder.

At a deep level, changes in a language are threatening because they signal widespread changes in social mores. At a level closer to the surface they are exasperating. We learn certain rules of grammar and usage in school, and when they are challenged it is as though we are also being challenged. Our native language is like a second skin, so much a part of us we resist the idea that it is constantly changing, constantly being renewed. Though we know intellectually that the English we speak today and the English of Shakespeare's time are very different, we tend to think of them as the same—static rather than dynamic. Emotionally, we want to agree with the syndicated columnist who wrote that "grammar is as fixed in its way as geometry."

One of the obstacles to accepting any kind of linguistic change —whether it concerns something as superficial as the pronunciation of *tomato* or as fundamental as sexual bias—is this desire to keep language "pure." In order to see change as natural and inevitable rather than as an affront, we need perspective, and to gain perspective it helps to take a look at some of the changes that have already taken place in English.

To start with, if it were true that "grammar is as fixed in its way as geometry," we would still, in the twentieth century, be speaking Old English, the earliest version of the tongue we know today: our vocabulary would be almost totally different; we would still be altering a word's form to change the meaning of a sentence instead of shifting words about—as in "Dog bites man," "Man bites dog"—to do the same thing; and we would still have "grammatical" rather than "natural" gender. The last change is important because the gender assigned to nouns and pronouns in Old English, as in most modern European languages, often had no relationship to sex or its absence. The word for "chair," for example, was masculine; the word for "table" was feminine; and the word for "ship" was neuter. In modern English we match gender with sex. That is, we reserve feminine and masculine gender for human beings and other sex-differentiated animals or, in flights of fancy, for nonliving things (like ships) onto which we project human associations. At least theoretically all other English nouns and pronouns are neuter or, in the case of agent-nouns like *teacher* and *president*, gender-neutral.

Greatly as these grammatical simplifications invigorated English, some of its special richness comes from the flexibility of its vocabulary. The English lexicon is a kind of uninhibited conglomeration put together over the centuries from related Indo-European languages and, though far less frequently, from languages as unrelated to English as Chinese, Nahuatl, and Yoruba.

Yet despite the hospitality of English to outside as well as internal influences, many people, including many language experts, become upset when confronted with new words or grammatical modifications they happen not to like. H. W. Fowler, whose widely used *Dictionary of Modern English Usage* was first published in 1926, deplored such "improperly formed" words as *amoral, bureaucrat, speedometer, pacifist,* and *coastal,* terms so commonly used today we take them for granted. His scorn for *electrocute* (formed by analogy to *execute*) pushed him beyond compassion or reason. The word, he wrote, "jars the unhappy latinist's nerves much more cruelly than the operation denoted jars those of its victims" (an emotional excess Sir Ernest Gowers, editor of the current edition of Fowler, mercifully deleted).

Lexicographers are less judgmental. In compiling dictionaries, they try to include as many commonly used words as space allows, whether the words are "properly formed" or not. Dictionaries, however, cannot help but lag behind actual usage, so they are not always reliable indicators of new or altered meanings. The 1986 edition of Webster's Ninth New Collegiate Dictionary defines *youth* as (among other things) "a young person; esp: a young male between adolescence and maturity." Essentially the same definition appears in several other current dictionaries, and some people continue to use the word in that limited sense. When film director Martha Coolidge approached a Hollywood producer about making a "low-budget youth picture," he is reported to have said, "No gays or women; it's a male subject." Actually the accepted meaning of *youth* is shifting faster than the producer realized or dictionaries can keep up with. Under the headline "Stolen Horse Is Found by Relentless Searcher," a news story in the *New York Times* referred to the horse's owner, a sixteen-year-old girl, as a youth: "After Rocky was stolen . . . the youth called every stable and horse handler she could find" and "the youth's parents brought a trailer . . . for the trip home." Though the term may once have been anomalous when used of a young woman, today it is a recognized common-gender noun, and the next round of dictionaries will no doubt add their authority to the change.

Changes in usage often occur slowly and imperceptibly, but some take place seemingly overnight. Such was the case in the 1960s when *black* replaced *Negro*. How the change occurred and something of the power of words was described by Shirley Chisholm:

> A few short years ago, if you called most Negroes "blacks," it was tantamount to calling us niggers. But now black is beauti-

ful, and black is proud. There are relatively few people, white or black, who do not recognize what has happened. Black people have freed themselves from the dead weight of albatross blackness that once hung around their necks. They have done it by picking it up in their arms and holding it out with pride for all the world to see. . . . [A]nd they have found that the skin that was once seen as symbolizing their chains is in reality their badge of honor.

Although a few people are still reluctant to accept this use of *black,* the balance has clearly shifted in its favor, and the familiar alternatives *Negro, colored,* and *Afro-American* are heard less often.

Ironically, those who deal with words professionally or avocationally can be the most resistant to linguistic changes. Like Fowler, they may know so much about etymology that any deviation from the classical pattern of word formation grates on their ears. Or having accepted certain rules of grammar as correct, they may find it impossible to acknowledge that those particular rules could ever be superseded.

What many people find hardest to accept is that a word which used to mean one thing now means another, and that continuing to use it in its former sense—no matter how impeccable its etymological credentials—can only invite misunderstanding. When the shift in meaning happened centuries ago, no problem lingers. One may be fully aware that *girl* once meant "a young person of either sex" (as it did in Chaucer's time) and yet not feel compelled to refer to a sexually mixed group of children as girls. When the change happens in one's lifetime, recognition and acceptance may be harder.

The word *intriguing* is such a case. Once understood to mean "conniving" or "deceitful" (as a verb, *intrigue* comes through the French *intriguer,* "to puzzle," from the Latin *intricare,* "to entangle"), *intriguing* now means "engaging the interest to a marked degree," as Webster's Third New International Dictionary noted over three decades ago. People still make statements like "They are an intriguing pair" with the intention of issuing a warning, but chances are the meaning conveyed is "They are a fascinating pair," because that is how a new generation of writers and speakers understands and uses the word. In one sense precision has been lost; in another it has only shifted.

The transformation of *man* over the past thousand years may be the most troublesome and significant change ever to overtake an English word. Once a synonym for "human being," *man* has gradually narrowed in meaning to become a synonym for "adult male human being" only. Put simply in the words of a popular dictionary for children, "A boy grows up to be a man. Father and Uncle George are both men." These are the meanings of *man* and *men* native speakers of English internalize because they are the meanings that from infancy on we hear applied in everyday speech. Though we may later acquire the information that *man* has another, "generic" meaning, we do not accept it with the same certainty that we accept the children's dictionary definition and its counterparts: A girl does not grow up to be a man. Mother and Aunt Teresa are not men; they are women.

To go on using in its former sense a word whose meaning has changed is counterproductive. The point is not that we should recognize semantic change, but that in order to be precise, in order to be understood, we must. The difference is a fundamental one in any discussion of linguistic bias, for some writers think their freedom of expression and artistic integrity are being compromised when they are asked to avoid certain words or grammatical forms. Is it ever justifiable, for example, for publishers to expect their authors to stop using the words *forefathers, man,* and *he* as though they were sex-inclusive? Is this not unwarranted interference with an author's style? Even censorship?

No, it is not. The public counts on those who disseminate factual information—especially publishers of textbooks and other forms of nonfiction, and those who work in the mass media—to be certain that what they tell us is as accurate as research and the conscientious use of language can make it. Only recently have we become aware that conventional English usage, including the generic use of masculine-gender words, often obscures the actions, the contributions, and sometimes the very presence of women. Turning our backs on that insight is an option, of course, but it is an option like teaching children that the world is flat. In this respect, continuing to use English in ways that have become misleading is no different from misusing data, whether the misuse is inadvertent or planned.

The need today, as always, is to be in command of language, not used by it, and so the challenge is to find clear, convincing, graceful ways to say accurately what we want to say. That is what this book attempts to do, and it begins, appropriately, with more on the meaning of *man.*

I believe the deeply rooted semantic confusion between "man" as a male and "man" as a species has been fed back into and vitiated a great deal of the speculation that goes on about the origins, development, and nature of the human race. . . . It's just as hard for man to break the habit of thinking of himself as central to the species as it was to break the habit of thinking of himself as central to the universe. He sees himself quite unconsciously as the main line of evolution, with a female satellite revolving around him as the moon revolves around the earth.

—Elaine Morgan, *The Descent of Woman*

1

Man as a False Generic

"Development of the Uterus in Rats, Guinea Pigs, and Men"

—Research report

Generic terms, like *rats* and *guinea pigs,* are equally applicable to a class or group and to its individual members. Terms used of a class or group that are not applicable to all its members are false generics. The reason the research-report title quoted above sounds incongruous is that the word *men* in that context does not apply to all members of the group it purports to designate. This was not always so, since *man* was once a true generic.

HISTORICAL BACKGROUND

Ercongota, the daughter of a seventh-century English king, is described in *The Anglo-Saxon Chronicle* as "a wonderful man." In Old English the word *man* meant "person" or "human being," and when used of an individual was equally applicable to either sex. It was parallel to the Latin *homo*, "a member of the human species," not *vir*, "an adult male of the species." English at the time of Ercongota had separate words to distinguish the sexes: *wer* (equivalent to the Latin *vir*) meant "adult male," and *wif* meant "adult female." The combined forms *waepman* and *wifman* meant, respectively, "adult male person" and "adult female person."

In the course of time *wifman* evolved into the modern word *woman*, and *wif* narrowed in meaning to become *wife* as we use that word today. *Man* eventually ceased to be used of individual women and replaced *wer* and *waepman* as a specific term distinguishing an adult male from an adult female. But *man* continued to be used in generalizations about both sexes. As long as most generalizations about people were made by men about men, the ambiguity nestling in this dual usage was either not noticed or thought not to matter.

By the eighteenth century the modern, narrow sense of *man* was firmly established as the predominant one. When Edmund Burke, writing of the French Revolution, used *men* in the old, inclusive way, he took pains to spell out his meaning: "Such a deplorable havoc is made in the minds of men (both sexes) in France. . . ." Thomas Jefferson did not make the same distinction in declaring that "all men are created equal" and "governments are instituted among men, deriving their just powers from the consent of the governed." In a time when women, having no vote, could neither give nor withhold consent, Jefferson had to be using the word *men* in its principal sense of "males," and it probably never occurred to him that anyone would think otherwise.

By the middle of the nineteenth century, most people in Great Britain and America apparently agreed with Jefferson that *man* is equivalent to *male*, at least in their interpretation of statute law. As part of his strategy on behalf of women's suffrage, John Stuart Mill proposed that the term *person* replace the term *man* in the Reform Bill of 1867, an Act of Parliament extending the franchise to certain males previously denied the vote. Today it is tantalizing to think of the difference that single change in terminology might have made.

Dictionaries still define *man* in both its narrow and broad senses. In the Random House College Dictionary, Revised Edition (1984), for example, the definition reads "1. an adult male person, as distinguished from a boy or woman. 2. the creature, *Homo sapiens*, at the highest level of animal development, characterized esp. by a highly developed brain. 3. the human race; mankind. . . ." The point at issue, therefore, is whether parts 2 and 3 of that definition are still fully operative or whether the first, limited meaning has, in effect, become the only valid one in modern English.

Studies of college students and school children (see **Reference Notes,** page 168) indicate that the broad definitions of *man* and *men,* although still taught, have to a significant degree become inoperative at a subliminal level. Phrases like *economic man* and *political man,* or statements like "Man domesticated animals" and "Man is a dreamer," it turns out, tend to call up images of male people only, not female people or females and males together.

Lexicographers appear to agree. Although they do not label the supposedly generic meaning of *man* obsolete, they write some definitions as though we all know it is. For example, Webster's Ninth New Collegiate Dictionary (1986) defines a man-about-town as "a worldly and socially active man." But if *man* sometimes means "any human being," should not the definition of *man-about-town* read "a worldly and socially active person of the male sex"? How can the definers be sure we will know without being told that a man-about-town is never a woman?

Lexicographers are aware, of course, that ever since English lost *waepman,* a specifically male-gender counterpart to *woman, man* has been shifting away from generality toward specificity. They also know that the limited meaning of *man* is the only one native speakers of English internalize as applying to an individual. Thus when Diana Nyad swam from Bimini to the Florida coast, the news media did not report that

> Marathon swimmer Diana Nyad became the first man
> to swim the 60 miles from the Bahamas to Florida.

They said, with incidental variations,

> "Marathon swimmer Diana Nyad became the first
> person to swim. . . ."

What lexicographers and grammarians are less attuned to is the extent to which this narrowing is felt. Because gender in modern English corresponds to sex or its absence, native speakers of the language increasingly sense the same contradiction in calling women "men" that they would feel in calling girls "boys" or daughters "sons." In reporting the remark of a member of Congress,

> " 'Every man on this subcommittee is for public
> works,' "

the *Wall Street Journal* appended a comment:

> "There are two women on the subcommittee and they
> are for public works, too."

Some writers tell themselves that they are using *man* in a generic sense when they spell it with an initial capital. The news columnist who wrote

> "In the tragedy of the Challenger, Man himself, homo
> sapiens, is the protagonist . . ."

even took pains to give his subject taxonomic identity. But linked with the prescriptive masculine-gender pronoun, the subject soon lost all pretense of inclusiveness, drowned in what has come to be known as the *he/man* syndrome:

> "Of this remarkable protagonist—Man—must it not be
> said that his capacity to adapt his universe and its
> physical laws to his own needs and desires and
> purposes—his science and technology—is one of the
> qualities of his greatness?"

Since capitalizing *man* only deifies the masculine image, the writer's message might have been stated more convincingly:

> In the tragedy of the Challenger, humanity itself is the
> protagonist. . . . Of this remarkable protagonist—
> homo sapiens—must it not be said that our capacity to
> adapt our universe and its physical laws to our own
> needs and desires and purposes—our science and
> technology—is one of the qualities of our species'
> greatness?

Writers who persist in using *man* in its old sense often slip
unconsciously from the general meaning to the limited one. The
switch, unfortunately, is rarely discernible to their readers, who
have no way of telling that generalizations about human beings
have become generalizations about males. Yet we know it does
happen—if not how often—because every once in a while an
author's unconscious lapse shows through, as in this example
from a book review:

> "[T]he book can be read with interest by people who
> . . . wonder about strange facts: why men speak and
> animals don't, why man feels so sad in the 20th
> century, why war is man's greatest pleasure."

Readers who assume "men speak" and "man feels so sad" refer
to all of us are brought up short by the final phrase. Whether
war is the greatest pleasure of most men is debatable, but would
anyone assert that it is the greatest pleasure of women?

Other lapses are even more revealing. One author, ostensibly
generalizing about all human beings, wrote:

> "As for man, he is no different from the rest. His back
> aches, he ruptures easily, his women have difficulties in
> childbirth. . . ."

If *man* and *he* were truly generic, the parallel phrase would have
been

> he has difficulties in childbirth.

And in a magazine article on aggression, where the context
indicated that *man* was supposed to include women, readers
were startled to come upon the statement

> "[M]an can do several things which the animal cannot
> do. . . . Eventually, his vital interests are not only life,
> food, access to females, etc., but also values, symbols,
> institutions. . . ."

In each case the narrow meaning of *man* had asserted itself,
leading the writer to equate the species with its male members.

Occasionally what seems to be the unintentional use of *man* in
both a generic and specific sense turns out to be the deliberate
use of the word in its narrow, modern meaning only—*man*
equals *male*. Elaine Morgan was playing that game when she
wrote

> "It's just as hard for man to break the habit of thinking
> of himself as central to the species as it was to break
> the habit of thinking of himself as central to the
> universe"

and then went on,

> "He sees himself . . . with a female satellite revolving
> around him. . . ."

A historian must have had fun writing

> "Suddenly, [John] Dewey's faith in the perfectibility of
> humanity gave way to belief in man's natural
> aggressiveness. And with the return of the awareness
> of aggression in man came a new enthusiasm for
> woman's nurturant qualities as a protection against his
> aggressive excesses."

Is the same degree of awareness also present in this use of
man by a third writer?

> "He gives us the voice of an imagined author, an
> author obsessed. Obsessed by what? . . . The
> malevolence of nature, the imperfectibility of man?
> The biblical contract between God and man? The
> traditional relation of man to wife?"

It hardly seems likely, but who can tell for sure?

As we know from modern psychology, man overlooks what
he does not want to see—and so does woman. But males have a

greater vested interest in preserving the way things were than in acknowledging the way they are. If the word *man* were not so emotionally charged and politically useful, its ambiguity would have led long ago to its disuse in any but the limited sense it immediately brings to mind. So the question for writers and speakers becomes, How can we get along without *man* in the old sense, that archaic crutch we no longer need but to which we have become habituated?

ALTERNATIVES TO "GENERIC" *MAN*

In Clichés

Compare the sentence

> When a shave and a haircut cost two bits, even the man in the street patronized a barber

with the sentence

> Though Mary Kilpatrick is already well known in the consumer advocacy movement, she'll need the support of the man in the street if she runs for office.

In the first, "the man in the street" clearly refers to males. In the second, the phrase is ambiguous. Perhaps the writer knows that Mary Kilpatrick already has a large following of women but needs the support of men. But does the reader know it? Phrases like *the common man* or *the average man* would have been equally unclear. Assuming the candidate needs the support of both women and men, the sentence could read:

> . . . she'll need a broad power base (*or* the support of ordinary voters *or* of the average voter) if she runs for office.

Another pair of sentences illustrates the lack of clarity in a cliché like *the working man:*

> The rich cannot possibly appreciate the impact of inflation on the average working man.

> The average working man earns almost twice as much
> as the average working woman.

The second example says what it means; one has no way of
knowing whether the author of the first had only males in mind
or was using English loosely. In either case, the sentence reveals
careless thinking that would have been corrected if the writer
had not used a false generic:

> The rich cannot possibly appreciate the impact of
> inflation on the average wage earner (*or* the average
> worker).

Generalizations about people couched in terms like *a man who,
if a man,* or *no man* are clearer when rephrased to include people
of both sexes (unless, of course, only males are intended). For
instance,

> A man who lies constantly needs a good memory

is clearer when *a man* is replaced by *someone* or *anyone.* Or better
still:

> A chronic liar needs a good memory.

Similar phrases, like

> If a man can drive 500 miles in ten hours . . .
>
> No man would be safe from nuclear fallout if . . .

can be recast in a variety of ways. For example:

> If someone (*or* If you *or* If one *or* If Jones) can
> drive . . .

or

> If it is possible to drive . . .
>
> No one (*or* No human being) would be safe from
> nuclear fallout if . . .

Terms for the Human Species

> " . . . it is now thought that a million years ago and
> more, earth was populated with more or less manlike

creatures, descended not from apes but from some forefather of both apes and men."

"The personal commitment of a man to his skill, the intellectual commitment and the emotional commitment working together as one, has made the Ascent of Man."

"Man has learned a lot. He has invented ever so many things. Someday you may even be able to go and visit the other planets."

Because scientists have traditionally "translated" the Latin term *Homo sapiens* as "man" rather than "human being," resistance to giving up this once-generic term is particularly strong in the scientific community. Those who write about anthropology and the biological sciences, including the authors of children's books on these subjects, are frequently addicted to using *man* in contexts like the above. From *near-man* through *early man* to *true man* and *modern man,* accounts of human evolution are couched in terms of *mankind* and *forefathers,* with frequent references to "his" cultural artifacts, the effect of erect posture in enabling "him" to see farther, "his" animals, crops, pottery, villages, etc., etc.

An entirely different image is projected in a story headlined "New Clues to Ancient Life" published in the newsletter *Indian Affairs*. Reporting on archaeological findings at the Koster site in Illinois, the writer, instead of relying on *man*, used such terms as *people, ancient people, residents of the ancient village, the site's inhabitants*, and *these early human populations*. The newsletter is a model of unbiased writing, and its commitment is evidently shared by the leader of the Koster exploration, archaeologist Stuart Struever, who is quoted in the article:

> "If we are to measure 'cultural success' in part by the ability of a human population to establish an equilibrium with its environment that can be sustained over the long haul, then these Koster residents were successful people, indeed."

Used in broad, sweeping generalizations, *man* frequently—perhaps usually—conveys misinformation.

> When ancient man developed agriculture . . .

rejects, as far as a listener or reader has any way of knowing, the extensive evidence now available indicating that women were the earliest cultivators of plants.

> Men have always hoped to conquer disease

appears not only to disregard women's interest in ending illness but also to ignore the important advances toward that goal made by women—from the anonymous healers and discoverers of curative plants to Nobel laureates. Authenticity is better served by phrases like

> When our ancestors (*or* people *or* human societies *or* our forebears) first developed agriculture . . .

> Human beings (*or* Men and women *or* Women and men) have always hoped to conquer disease.

Sometimes the best solution is to rephrase a thought completely:

> The conquest of disease has always been a goal of human societies.

Biblical translations into English have traditionally used *man* in passages where the wording of the original text could have been rendered inclusively. The familiar language of Matthew 4:4, for example,

> "Man shall not live by bread alone,"

is made more consistent with the Greek text and reflects contemporary usage more accurately when phrased

> "One does not live by bread alone,"

as is the case in the *Revised New Testament of the New American Bible,* published in 1987 and authorized for use by Roman Catholics in the United States.

The historian Mary Beard pointed out many years ago that most historians use *man* in ways that obscure women's contributions to civilization. Unfortunately they, and others, continue to do so. The list of books with titles like *Man and His Symbols, The Condition of Man, The Identity of Man, Man's Unconquerable Mind, The Family of Man, The Tree Where Man Was Born,* and *Man Must Speak* appears to be endless. Dale Spender parodies these misnomers with her title *Man Made Language,* a book that shows how meanings and definitions in male-dominated society have helped structure and maintain women's subordination. And Stephen Jay Gould clinched the case against the "generic" *man* trap when he called his historical survey of racist, sexist, and class bias in certain areas of science *The Mismeasure of Man.* In an introductory note, Gould explained the book's title:

> I hope that an apparently sexist title will be taken in the intended spirit—not only as a play on Protagoras' famous aphorism, but also as a commentary on the procedures of biological determinists discussed in the book. They did, indeed, study "man" (that is, white European males), regarding this group as a standard and everybody else as something to be measured unfavorably against it. That they mismeasured "man" underscores the double fallacy.

Men of Letters and Other Women

> "The history of every country begins in the heart of a
> man or a woman."

Willa Cather expressed that conviction at the end of a moving
passage in *O Pioneers!* As a woman writing about a woman, she
was not likely to fall into the trap set by the false generic *man*. A
noted sculptor was less in tune with reality when he said

> "A work of art is beautiful because a man did it."

One assumes he did not mean to exclude a sculpture by Louise
Nevelson or a painting by Georgia O'Keeffe, yet his choice of
words betrayed him into doing so. Though one can only guess,
it may be that he meant something like

> A work of art is beautiful because a human being
> created it.

Unintentional exclusion is hard to distinguish from inten-
tional exclusion. Did a book reviewer who described George
Will as

> "the principal public philosopher and man of letters of
> our generation"

mean to exclude, let us say, Susan Sontag? If he had called Will

> the principal public philosopher and writer of our
> generation

that particular question would not have come up.

Women in art, in science, in education, and in business and
politics are adding a dimension to the human environment that
was previously lacking. As Hanna Holborn Gray, president of
the University of Chicago, said in a baccalaureate address:

> "The institution of the university is not, in Emerson's
> phrase, the lengthened shadow of one man, but rather
> that of many men and women who care for its
> purposes."

If Gray had said

> The institution of the university is not, in Emerson's phrase, the lengthened shadow of one man, but rather of many men who care for its purposes

she would have conveyed a different message, even if in her own mind she intended the word *men* to be understood inclusively.

Man as a Verb

The verb *to man* comes from the noun and dates from the Middle English period when it was used in the sense of furnishing a ship or fort or castle with men to operate or defend it. By analogy *man* came to be used in the sense of "to work at," as in "to man" a production line or information booth (though seldom, if ever, a tea table). *Work, staff, serve at (on), operate,* and other alternatives can be used instead of *man:*

They had to man the pumps all night.	They had to work the pumps all night.
The Girl Scouts will man the exhibit.	The Girl Scouts will run the exhibit.
The emergency room must be manned at all times.	The emergency room must be staffed (*or* covered) at all times.
Man the barricades!	Mount the barricades! (*or* To the barricades!)

Man's Inhumanity to Men

Men as well as women are often stereotyped in ways that seem unfair. "Doorman and trashman spread the idea that only men are appropriate for these lowly jobs," the journalist Jack Kammer points out. "And every time there is violence the news reports always refer to a gunman . . . even if the person was masked and nobody really knows." Kammer wants to know why reporters don't use the words *robber* or *intruder* instead of *gun-*

man, and *trash collector* instead of *trashman*—to which any woman conscious of the restricting power of labels can only say Amen.

Several organizations, among them Men's Rights Inc., based in Boston and Sacramento, and the Fathers Rights Association of New York State, take this problem very seriously, but are they taking it seriously enough? Males are often accorded sole credit for great human accomplishments attributed to *man,* but they also often get sole blame for history's horrors. Whether the writers quoted below were visualizing males only, or females and males, is anybody's guess—though it need not have been, as the rewritten versions show.

" . . . why should [visitors from space] not see the same virtues in domesticating human beings that men realized long ago when they domesticated cattle, horses, dogs and cats? Or impressed other human beings into slavery?"

. . . why should [visitors from space] not see the same virtues in domesticating human beings that humans themselves realized long ago when they domesticated cattle, horses, dogs and cats? Or impressed their fellow humans into slavery?

"Muir knew that man's spirit can only survive in a land that is spacious and unpolluted. . . . He felt that man should come as a visitor to these places—the mountains, river canyons, coasts, deserts and swamps —to learn, not to leave his mark."

Muir knew that the human spirit can only survive in a land that is spacious and unpolluted. . . . He felt that we should come as visitors to these places . . . to learn, not to leave our mark.

"Man should be presented [to children] as a steward of the animals rather than the 'most intelligent' creature who has the right to do as he pleases with the other animals."

People (*or* the human race) should be presented [to children] as stewards of the animals rather than the 'most intelligent' of creatures with the right to do as we please with the other animals.

"[Hart] Crane seems to have believed that daily life enforced a sufficient degree of penance and that a man had the right to make the best of it, taking his pleasures where he found them."

Crane seems to have believed that daily life enforced a sufficient degree of penance and that we all have the right to make the best of it, taking our pleasures where we find them.

SHALL WE LET THEM KEEP THIS ONE ?

Anyone who chooses to use *man* in its old, generic sense can claim centuries of precedent. But even centuries of precedent crumble if those on the receiving end hear a different meaning from the one intended. When Edith Bunker, on the television series "All in the Family," quoted Sam Walter Foss's

"Let me live in my house by the side of the road
And be a friend of man,"

Archie's response was,

"Yeah, I heard about them kind of houses in the
Army."

MAN IN COMPOUNDS

"America's manpower begins with boy power."

"The annual exhibit of the Connecticut Society of Craftsmen—which includes women artists as well—opens Thursday. . . ."

The exclusion and ambiguity characteristic of *man* when it is used generically extend to compound words like *manpower* and *craftsman*. Before discussing such words, however, it is important to note that *woman* and *human* are not, as is often implied, compounds incorporating the modern word *man*. *Woman* is a combination of *wif*, meaning "an adult female," and *man* in its lost sense of "a human being irrespective of sex or age." *Human* is from the Latin *humanus*, akin to *homo*, also meaning "human being." Neither has any more relation to a word originally meaning "male person" than do words like *manager*, *manufacture*, *manuscript*, and *manipulate*, which come from the Latin *manus*, "hand." The most that can be said about the belabored form of ridicule which suggests we must find alternatives for every word containing the syllable *man* is that *wobody*, *huperson*, *personipulate*, etc., are ideas whose time has gone.

Man as a Prefix

"Should all despair that have revolted wives, the tenth of mankind would hang themselves."
                                        —William Shakespeare

"The infinite simplicity and silliness of mankind and womankind. . . ."
                                        —Anthony Trollope

"When I speak of mankind, one thing I *don't* mean is womankind."
                                        —Man in a Steig cartoon

For more than four centuries *mankind* has been used, as in the examples above, to differentiate men from women. To avoid ambiguity and occasional ineptness, as in

> The Pap test, which has greatly reduced mortality from uterine cancer, is a boon to mankind,

alternative terms that clearly designate people as distinguished from other forms of life can be useful:

> The Pap test, which has greatly reduced mortality from uterine cancer, is a boon to humanity (*or* humankind).

An even more serious drawback to *mankind* when used to mean people collectively is that, willy-nilly, like *man*, it imposes the image of maleness on the entire species—which in turn often fosters an androcentric view of the rest of nature.

> "Will mankind murder Mother Earth or will he redeem her?"

asks a historian. The effect of the question may be less dramatic when the imagery of male aggressor and female victim is removed, but since such stereotypical behavior has failed to benefit humanity in the past, rewording the question might suggest at least part of the answer:

> Will human beings destroy the earth's life-sustaining environment or will they rescue it?

Speakers and writers often use *man*-prefixed compounds in contexts where *man* represents males alone or both males and females, but they tend to avoid such compounds as incongruous when the subjects are explicitly female.

> The only water supply is a manmade pond, which the villagers created by damming a small stream

conveys an assumption of male involvement. If the writer knew the dam had been built entirely by women, the sentence might have read:

> The only water supply is an artificial pond, which the women of the village created by damming a small stream.

When explaining whether something has been made by women, men, or both is irrelevant—and it usually is—various sex-neutral alternatives to *manmade* are available, including *handmade, hand-built, synthetic, manufactured, fabricated, machine-made,* and *constructed:*

> The cave appears to be natural, but it was completely excavated by hand (*or* built by hand *or* hand-built).

> All materials in these shoes are synthetic (*or* manufactured).

> Since the showcase is only 2 feet deep, the illusion of great depth is simulated (*or* cleverly created).

The art critic and historian Lucy Lippard wrote:

> "When I cross a moor on which no tree, habitation, or person is visible, and come upon a ring of ragged stones, a single rough-hewn pillar, a line curving away over a hill . . . I know this is human-made."

Sometimes a sentence can be recast to omit the adjective entirely, as in this version of the "manmade pond" example:

> The only water supply is a pond the villagers created by damming a small stream.

When Bryan Allen pedaled his way across the English Channel in the *Gossamer Albatross* some years ago, most news reports used the term *manpowered flight.* Perhaps with the thought that a future air cyclist would be a woman, *Time* magazine came up with

> "muscle-powered flight,"

and Doug Tunnell referred on CBS News to

> "human-powered flight,"

a term most of the media had adopted by 1987, when Lois McCallin established a new record pedaling the *Eagle* over a desert course in California.

*　　　　*　　　　*

In some contexts a compound like *manpower* clearly excludes females, as in the slogan "America's manpower begins with boy power." On the other hand, an employment agency called Manpower® Temporary Services contracts for per diem secretaries and typists, most of whom are women. Outside the world of registered trademarks, *manpower* is usually replaceable with *personnel, staff, work force, available workers,* or *human resources,* as in:

With the signing of the new contracts our manpower needs will double.	With the signing of the new contracts our personnel needs will double.
"Although the FDA hasn't yet formally responded to the petition, agency officials say they don't have enough manpower to give the noodle issue a high priority."	. . . agency officials say they don't have enough staff to give the noodle issue a high priority.
The development of alternative forms of energy requires both technology and manpower.	The development of alternative forms of energy requires both technology and human resources.
"A study of nursing manpower is in progress."	A study of available nurses (*or* the nursing work force) is in progress.

It is worth noting in this connection that the former Manpower Administration of the United States Department of Labor has been renamed. The new name, which better characterizes the organization's function, is the Employment and Training Administration.

Man-hour is an imprecise term at best, especially when one man's hour may be another man's or woman's 45 minutes. If a unit of work is measured according to the time the average worker takes to do it, why not call it a *work-hour*? Or the name of the job may suggest another alternative:

Direct dialing saves the telephone company millions of man-hours.	Direct dialing saves the telephone company millions of operator-hours.

As for *manhole cover,* judging from the frequency with which opponents of nonsexist language refer to "personhole covers," vast numbers of people across the English-speaking world must have developed a consuming interest in the plates that keep them from falling into sewers, water mains, conduits, boilers, etc. As a last defense against reason, the "personhole-cover" issue may persist for years. In the meantime, anyone who needs an accurate term for the covers of utility holes might try either *access covers* or *utility-hole covers,* as in

> The boiler's access cover, which is usually bolted in place, had been removed.

> The explosion blew a utility-hole cover 10 feet into the air.

Man as a Suffix

A few usage critics maintain that compounds ending in un-accented *man* are always sex-neutral: *layman, tradesman, fisherman.* (At least one linguist has suggested, perhaps facetiously, that generic interpretation of these words can best be assured by spelling them as they are pronounced, m-u-n.) More often, however, arbiters of usage assign generic status in some instances and not in others—and their reasons are usually hard to discern.

The New York Times Manual of Style and Usage (1982) offers a number of examples. Although it proscribes both *spokeswoman* and *spokesperson,* it permits the use of *saleswoman,* which may be an indication that whoever makes such decisions thinks *salesman* applies to males only. Why anyone should decide it is all right for women to be called "saleswomen" but not "spokeswomen" is unclear. Not only have both terms been in use for some three hundred years, but the earliest citation for *spokeswoman* provided by the Oxford English Dictionary is dated 1654, fifty years before the dictionary's first citation for *saleswoman*.

Without a logical basis for their decision, and with both common sense and common usage pointing the other way, even the *Times* seems to have had trouble keeping its troops in line. Or perhaps the word has finally been passed that—at least with reference to terms ending in -*man*—the *Manual* would be more honored in the breach than in the observance; for although female "spokesmen" and "chairmen" continue to appear in the pages of the *Times*, items like the following are becoming equally, if not more, common:

> "A hospital spokesperson said Doe's injuries were 'nothing too critical.' "

> "Margarita Mathiopoulos . . . was offered a post as party spokeswoman."

The *Associated Press Stylebook* (revised 1986), which approves *spokeswoman* but not *spokesperson*, suggests that writers use *representative* when the sex of the individual is not known.

> A representative of the corporation will meet with the press at 4 P.M.

The *Man* in the Chair

For some reason, what to call the person who heads an academic department or chairs a committee or meeting arouses great anxiety. *Chairman*, according to the same New York Times style manual, "suffices for both sexes," and so the *Times* still officially frowns on both *chairwoman* and *chairperson*. But since everyone knows that style manuals are no sooner published than they tend to become embarrassingly passé, it is not surprising that a generous sprinkling of *chairwomen* now appear in *Times* news reports, as in

> "Mrs. Pelosi, 47, a liberal former state party chairwoman and 1986 national finance chairwoman of the Democratic Senatorial Campaign Committee, is the candidate."

Unfortunately, it will take more than a majority of the English-speaking world's newspapers to convince the National Association of Parliamentarians that *chairman* is not appropriate when used of a woman, and a sizable number of individuals take the same position. When an editor changed the word *chairman* to *chairperson* in an article written by an unnamed friend of the columnist William F. Buckley, Buckley was sufficiently upset to write a piece about it. It seems his friend telephoned the editor who had made the change, and the following conversation ensued, as reported by Buckley: "Where do you get off putting 'chairperson' where I specified 'chairman'? Well, she said, it's just this simple, you were talking about a woman. To which he replied that it was just this simple, namely that 'chairman' refers, and has done so for hundreds of years, equally to men as to women. . . ."

William Buckley's friend spoke with the certainty of the righteously indignant, but can he back up his claim that *chairman* has referred equally to both sexes for "hundreds of years"? According to the Oxford English Dictionary, *chairman* has been used since at least 1654 and *chairwoman* since 1699. In each of the seventeenth-century quotations the dictionary provides to illustrate *chairman,* the person referred to was clearly male, and none of the citations from later periods shows the use of this word for a female. What the dictionary clearly documents is that for hundreds of years most -*man* compounds were recognized as applying only to men, just as -*woman* compounds applied only to women: terms like *gentleman, countryman, layman,* and *statesman* had their counterparts in *gentlewoman, countrywoman, laywoman,* and *stateswoman*; and women who worked as launderers and cleaners were known as *washerwomen, charwomen,* and *scrubwomen,* not *washermen, charmen,* and *scrubmen.*

The care with which nineteenth-century writers indicated sex in their use of compound -*man* and -*woman* terms is demonstrated by no less a litterateur than William Dean Howells. In an essay written in 1886, Howells said of the playwright Edward Harrigan,

> "Mr. Harrigan shows us the streetcleaners and
> contractors, the grocery men, the shysters, the

politicians, the washerwomen, the servant girls, the truckmen, the policemen, the risen Irishman and Irishwoman of contemporary New York."

Since the current aversion to using *woman* in compounds like *chairwoman* and *spokeswoman* cannot be attributed to lack of precedent, is there some other explanation? Perhaps *chairwoman* sounds less important and *spokeswoman* less authoritative than their masculine-gender counterparts. This could explain why some women who achieve positions of leadership still call themselves "chairmen," a term already invested with prestige and power by generations of male incumbents. Or could it be that at least some women go along with the unconscious desire of some men to keep terms like *chairman, alderman,* and *congressman* "official," thereby guarding a traditional male bailiwick from outsiders?

Whatever the reasons for its disfavor, *chairwoman* is a historically sound parallel to *chairman,* and it pays a woman the courtesy of recognizing both her sex and her achievement. It does not, however, solve the problem of what to use as an indefinite, sex-inclusive title. Instead of the much maligned but persistent *chairperson,* some groups and institutions have chosen to use entirely different titles like *presider, presiding officer, coordinator,* and *convener.*

A more obvious solution, the word *chair,* is used increasingly by governing bodies, organizations, and universities:

"The new Speaker of the House has not yet selected committee chairs."

"Dr. Roe served as program chair at last year's convention."

"Harry Coe has been named chair of the English Department."

The lexicographer Alma Graham points out that *chair* has been recognized, in the sense of "the occupant of the chair . . . as invested with its dignity," since the seventeenth century, just as *the Crown* has been used for the monarch, or *the Oval Office* has come to stand for the President of the United States. "Address your remarks to the chair" illustrates metonymy, a figure of speech in which something is called by the name of something else associated with it. Nobody understands an injunction to "address the chair" as an order to talk to a piece of furniture.

Groups of People as *Men*

Sometimes what makes a masculine-gender suffix inappropriate is not that the sex of an individual has been misrepresented, but that the reference is to many individuals of both sexes. Pauli Murray faced that problem in her autobiography when referring to one branch of her ancestry, and she solved it handily:

> "I haven't the slightest notion of who my particular African ancestors were . . . whether they were traders, fisherfolk, herdspeople, or farmers. . . ."

Africans, Italians, Russians, Japanese, Pakistanis, and *Australians,* to pick some random examples, can refer to either females or males. In contrast, terms like *Englishmen, Frenchmen,* and *Irishmen* are ambiguous if used nonspecifically.

> Englishmen are said to prefer tea to coffee

presumably means

> The English are said to prefer tea to coffee

whereas

> Englishmen are said to prefer blonds

is probably intended to refer to the preferences of males. Tom Brokaw of NBC News, introducing a report on the plight of a diminishing group of nomadic hunters and gatherers of South Africa, avoided possible misinterpretation by referring to

> "the struggle to save one tiny band of Bushpeople."

Precedent for terms like *laywoman* and *stateswoman* as counterparts to *layman* and *statesman* is well documented, as already mentioned (see page 32). Plural forms, when the group specified includes both sexes, may be somewhat more recalcitrant, but they yield, and in the process ambiguity is avoided:

"Obviously few laymen are knowledgeable enough to effectively judge the qualifications of an anesthesiologist."

Obviously few lay people are knowledgeable enough . . .
or
Obviously special training is needed to effectively judge the qualifications of an anesthesiologist.

The show includes the work of craftsmen from every state.

The show includes the work of craftspeople (*or* artisans) from every state.

(See also **Fellow,** pages 133–134, for a discussion of *fellowman.*)

Public *Man*servants

Congressman, assemblyman, councilman, selectman, etc., originated as masculine-gender designations when women's participation in the councils of government was, with rare exceptions like a queen's, unheard of, even unthinkable. In the words of Thomas Jefferson,

> Were our State a pure democracy, in which all its inhabitants should meet together to transact all their business, there would yet be excluded from their deliberations, 1. Infants, until arrived at years of discretion. 2. Women, who, to prevent depravation of morals and ambiguity of issue, could not mix promiscuously in the public meetings of men. 3. Slaves, from whom the unfortunate state of things with us takes away the right of will and of property.

Now that women's participation in government on an equal basis with men is no longer unthinkable, the use of new terms like *congresswoman, assemblywoman, councilwoman,* and *selectwoman* shows that the older titles were not sex-neutral, and that they remain designations appropriate only for males.

New sex-inclusive language is emerging, however. Present alternatives to the false generic *congressman* include *member of Con-*

gress and *representative,* and no doubt other ways will also evolve to designate those elected to offices that were once male domains. A member of a council, city or otherwise, is a *councillor,* for example. In line with the ancient linguistic process whereby adjectives are converted into nouns, a member of Congress may someday be simply a *congressional,* just as a member of a nation is a *national.*

Job Titles

Like the titles of public offices, most job titles ending in *man* date from a time when only males performed the jobs described. It was natural to speak of an *insurance man, delivery man, draftsman,* or *newsboy* because, with the possible exception of *businessman,* the masculine-gender terms matched the sex of nearly everyone doing the jobs described.

Not so today: girls have newspaper delivery routes, and women sell insurance, deliver packages, draft structural plans, and run successful businesses, making the old job titles, when retained, discriminatory. If a job category is labeled *lineman* or *repairman,* for instance, whoever does the hiring may look on the job as unsuitable for a woman. Furthermore, employers who use sex-differentiating titles like *salesman* and *saleswoman,* or *forelady* and *foreman,* often adopt two separate pay scales for the same work and pay their male employees more. Although to comply with the law employers carefully advertise positions as being open to both sexes, some keep the old sex-labeled titles. These titles act as a code, psychologically inhibiting women from applying for such jobs as *kennelman, stockman,* or *busboy,* and men from applying for jobs with titles ending in *woman, lady,* or *-ess.*

Similarly, job titles like *hat-check girl* and *junior executive,* which imply that youth is a prerequisite for the job, encourage age discrimination on the part of employers and can deter older people from applying.

In response to such considerations, the United States Department of Labor has revised its *Dictionary of Occupational Titles* to eliminate sex- and age-referent language. The dictionary, a volume of some 1,400 pages to which supplements are issued periodically, is available at many public libraries. A related book,

the *Occupational Outlook Handbook,* published by the department's Bureau of Labor Statistics, describes jobs in nearly every
field of employment, also using sex-neutral language throughout. Some of the Department of Labor's job title changes are:

From	To
airline steward, stewardess	flight attendant
cameraman, camera girl	camera operator
charwoman	charworker
draftsman	drafter
fisherman	fisher
forelady, foreman	supervisor
gateman	gate attendant
hat-check girl	hat-check attendant
junior executive	executive trainee
laundress, laundryman	laundry worker
lineman	line installer, line repairer
longshoreman	stevedore
maid	house worker
pressman	press operator
repairman	repairer
salesman	sales agent, sales associate
seamstress	sewer, mender
watchman	guard

There are other alternatives, of course, for anyone not limited
to the titles used in official job descriptions. Since writers and
speakers often need variety to avoid monotonous repetition,
additional possibilities are suggested in the **Brief Thesaurus**
beginning on page 155.

The serious impact of occupational terminology has been acknowledged by state governments as well, many of which have
changed the term *workmen's compensation* to *workers' compensation*
in their official documents and publications. *Worker* is also useful as a suffix, as in *longshoreworker* for *longshoreman.* That particular term is a shortening of "along shore," making *worker* a
logical addition, and since no one thinks titles like *garmentworker,*
steelworker, and *pieceworker* sound funny, why should *longshore-*
worker? Resistance to such terms as *repairer* (for *repairman*) and

launderer (for *laundress* and *laundryman*) is also odd considering the frequency of *-er* and *-or* endings in other agent-nouns: *explorer, bookkeeper, helper, lawyer, painter, photographer, laborer, auditor, conductor,* etc.

With some compounds ending in *man,* the solution of simply dropping the last syllable revives a former usage that proves to be still serviceable. *Watchman,* for instance, can become *watch,* used from the sixteenth to the nineteenth centuries to mean "one who watches . . . for the purposes of guarding and protecting life and property."

Alternatives to *salesman, saleswoman,* and their plurals are numerous, including the long-accepted *salesperson:*

> Ask any salesperson for help if you don't find what you need.

> Our salespeople (*or* agents *or* brokers) have a weekly conference.

> He was a sales representative for IBM before coming here.

> The sales force (*or* sales staff) is being reorganized.

> We'll need more salesclerks for the Christmas season.

Anyone who adamantly rejects *person* as a suffix (see **Person,** (page 146) has the option of using *foreman* or *forewoman* when speaking of a jury, or they can come up with a new term like *head juror* or *jury leader;* when the reference is to someone in charge of factory or construction workers, *supervisor, boss,* or *job boss* are alternatives to *forelady, forewoman,* and *foreman.*

Weatherman, newsman, anchorman, and similar designations in which the *man* ending is clearly accented have never been considered sex-inclusive, and women in these posts are usually assigned other job titles. During the 1950s, women who replaced men as television weather reporters were called "weather girls" (although their predecessors had not been called "weather boys"). The common-gender *weather people* may evoke shades of the Weather Underground for some, but there are other possibilities:

Channel 5 hired a new weathercaster last month,

A weather reporter's popularity rating is likely to go up
and down with the weather,

or, where the title describes the trained specialist,

The article was written by a meteorologist on the staff
of the National Weather Service.

Newsman and *anchorman* are easily made sex-inclusive:

You are invited to send a reporter (*or* news
representative *or* newscaster) to the launching.

The Journalist of the Year Award will be announced
next Tuesday.

Who will get the job of anchor on the six o'clock news?

Although many common-gender job titles have been readily
accepted and are being used routinely, others are resisted by
people in the occupations specified. For example, some individuals and organizations in the fishing industry, including some
women, objected when the National Marine Fisheries Service
began to use *fisher* instead of *fisherman* in its reports and correspondence. According to news stories, the objectors held that
the term *fisherman* "has a long and proud history dating back
thousands of years." In fact, *fisherman* entered the English language only in the sixteenth century, according to the Oxford
English Dictionary, whereas *fisher* was used in the ninth century
to mean "a person who fishes," and it appears many times in
that sense in the King James Version of the Bible. (*Fishermen*
appears only once.) *Fisher* is also used in references to sports
fishing, as in a *New York Times* piece by Enid Nemy:

"Ms. Bockman . . . is, as might be guessed, an ardent
fly fisher."

Fortunately, the desire of some people who fish to be called
"fishermen" can be respected in individual communication
without subverting the purpose of sex-neutral occupational titles. The significance of the new terms is that ultimately a

younger generation can grow up free from limiting concepts of "men's jobs" and "women's jobs."

It would be impossible to include in this section all the compound job titles ending in *man* for which common-gender alternatives are needed and are being sought. The examples given are intended to suggest the scope of the problem and the kinds of solutions available. ***Writers and speakers who are willing to experiment and perhaps come up with their own new terms or compounds will risk the wrath of language purists, but they will be in the company of many respected writers who have added to the vitality of English.***

Some Recalcitrant Compounds

When the *man* syllable comes in the middle of a word, finding a one-word alternative is hard. No one seriously suggests *sportsmanship* should be turned into *sportspersonship,* and as an alternative for *workmanlike, workerlike,* though passable, lacks force. Fortunately, synonyms can usually be found:

The award is for sportsmanship.	The award is for the highest ideals of fair play.
The bricklayers did a workmanlike job.	The bricklayers did a skillful job *or* The bricklayers' work was well done.
Their statesmanlike actions were commendable.	Their diplomatic actions (*or* tact and skill) were commendable.

FATHERS, BROTHERS, AND BOMFOG

To describe George Washington as "the father of his country" or to speak of the authors of the United States Constitution as "the Founding Fathers" is to use sexually appropriate metaphors. But to lump all the people who came over on the *Mayflower* under the name "Pilgrim Fathers" is nonsense. Women and girls were members of the company, and the survival of the new colony depended as much on them as on their male companions. Why not simply call them all Pilgrims?

Similarly, although *Christian Fathers* is a specialized term that refers to particular men in the early church, it is inappropriate to speak of the "fathers of industry" or the "fathers of industrial medicine." The latter phrase excludes, for example, Dr. Alice Hamilton, acknowledged leader in that field, and the former ignores the inventive genius of women like Catherine Littlefield Greene, who suggested the need for a cotton gin to Eli Whitney and who may have contributed substantially to its design; Margaret E. Knight, a nineteenth-century inventor of industrial machinery; and unknown numbers of anonymous women whose creative ideas were credited to men. Common-gender nouns like *pioneers, founders, trailblazers,* and *innovators* are useful alternatives to the metaphorical "fathers" who were female as well as male.

SALLY FORTH   BY GREG HOWARD

Like *fathers*, the words *brothers, brethren,* and *brotherhood* are masculine-gender terms with standard feminine-gender equivalents. Generations of sisters have been expected to accept the use of *brother* terms as symbols of universal human kinship—theirs not to question why. Yet the questions remain. Does a carpenter become a "brother" when she joins a trade union calling itself a "Brotherhood"? Who is invited to take part in

National Brotherhood Week? Does a billboard proclaiming that "Love Transforms Us into Brothers" mean to suggest a new approach to sex change?

"The brotherhood of man and the fatherhood of God" sounds noble—until one thinks about the people it leaves out. A few years ago reporters covering political campaigns heard the phrase so often they recorded it in their notes by initials only: BOMFOG. Shorthand for all the false generic terms and expressions that define women as nonhuman, BOMFOG, in the words of the author Eve Merriam, "continues to engulf our language and distort our thinking."

Language is our means of classifying and ordering the world. . . . and if it is inherently inaccurate, then we are misled. If the rules which underlie our language system, our symbolic order, are invalid, then we are daily deceived.

—Dale Spender, *Man Made Language*

[W]e have this notion of "the language" as a hallowed institution whose traditions may not be queried. . . . This picture of language as something external, independent and disinterested stops us asking whose language it is, whose traditions will be under attack if the conventions are changed. . . . It is not good enough to shrug our shoulders and say that male bias in usage is purely grammatical, and that therefore it does not matter.

—Deborah Cameron, *Feminism and Linguistic Theory*

2

The Pronoun Problem

"God send everyone their heart's desire."

Most people are taught in school that the above sentence is ungrammatical. It should be corrected, we are told, to read

God send everyone his heart's desire.

Use of the pronouns *he, his,* and *him* to refer to any unspecified or hypothetical person who may be either female or male is usually justified on two grounds. First, the practice is said to be an ancient rule of English grammar long and faithfully followed by educated speakers and writers. Second, it is asserted—somewhat paradoxically, if the usage is thought to distinguish the educated from the uneducated—that everybody knows *he* includes *she* in generalizations. Historical and psychological research in the past few years has produced evidence to refute both claims.

HISTORICAL BACKGROUND

The first grammars of modern English were written in the sixteenth and seventeenth centuries. They were mainly intended to help boys from well-to-do families prepare for the study of Latin, a language most scholars considered superior to English. The male authors of these earliest English grammars wrote for male readers in an age when few women were literate. The masculine-gender pronouns they used in grammatical examples and generalizations did not reflect a belief that masculine pronouns could refer to both sexes. They reflected the reality of male cultural dominance and the male-centered world view that resulted. Males were perceived as the standard representatives of the human species, females as something else.

Although the early grammarians examined many aspects of their native tongue and framed innumerable rules governing its use, their writings contain no statement to the effect that masculine pronouns are sex-inclusive when used in general references. Not until the eighteenth century did a "rule" mandating such usage appear in an English grammar book, and not until the nineteenth century was it widely taught.

Present-day linguists, tracing the history of the so-called generic *he*, have found that it was invented and prescribed by the grammarians themselves in an attempt to change long-established English usage. The object of the grammarians' intervention was the widespread acceptance of *they* as a singular pronoun, as in Lord Chesterfield's remark (1759),

> "If a person is born of a gloomy temper . . . they
> cannot help it."

Nearly three centuries earlier, England's first printer, William Caxton, had written,

> "Each of them should . . . make themself ready,"

and the invocation

"God send everyone their heart's desire"

is from Shakespeare. In such usages, grammarians argued, *they* lacked the important syntactical feature of agreement in number with a singular antecedent. But in prescribing *he* as the alternative, they dismissed as unimportant a lack of agreement in gender with a feminine antecedent.

In 1850 an Act of Parliament gave official sanction to the recently invented concept of the "generic" *he*. In the language used in acts of Parliament, the new law said, "words importing the masculine gender shall be deemed and taken to include females." Although similar language in contracts and other legal documents subsequently helped reinforce this grammatical edict in all English-speaking countries, it was often conveniently ignored. In 1879, for example, a move to admit female physicians to the all-male Massachusetts Medical Society was effectively blocked on the grounds that the society's by-laws describing membership used the pronoun *he*.

As a linguistic device imposed on the language rather than a natural development arising from a broad consensus, the "generic" *he* is fatally flawed. This fact has been demonstrated in several recent systematic investigations of how people of both sexes use and understand personal pronouns. (See **Reference Notes,** page 170.) The studies confirm that in spoken usage— from the speech of young children to the conversation of university professors—*he* is rarely intended or understood to include *she*. On the contrary, at all levels of education people whose native tongue is English seem to know that *he, him,* and *his* are gender-specific and cannot do the double duty asked of them.

The limitation of the "generic" pronoun was nicely illustrated by C. Badendyck, who wrote to the *New York Times Magazine* in response to William Safire's assertion that it is "O.K. to say 'Everyone should watch his pronoun agreement.' " Said Badendyck:

> Knowing that *he* and *his* can be gender neutral, I shall no longer feel there is an odd image filtering through something

> like: "The average American needs the small routines of get-
> ting ready for work. As he shaves or blow-dries his hair or
> pulls on his panty hose, he is easing himself by small stages
> into the demands of the day." . . . How liberating common
> sense can be.

The failure of masculine-generic pronouns to represent everyone is also apparent when the referent of the pronoun is sure
to be a woman, as in:

> "I myself don't object to *Everyone raised his voice in song*
> (unless we're referring to a female choir)."

When it comes to generalizations about secretaries, nurses,
and preschool teachers, the pronoun traditionally used is *she*.
But in such cases, as well as in *The New Yorker*'s response to the
following goof made by a newspaper reporter, *she* and its de-
clined forms are also false generics:

> "Meals are prepared under supervision of a dietician
> packaged in disposable Styrofoam containers."

To which *The New Yorker* replied,

> "Never mind her predicament. Are the meals any
> good?"

Why not "his predicament," if masculine pronouns are really
generic when used of an unspecified person? Because, grammarians to the contrary, *he* brings a male image to mind, and it
does so whether choir members, acrobats, nomads, or dieticians
are the subjects. And let's face it: male dieticians packaged in
Styrofoam are not thought to be as good for a laugh as female
dieticians packaged in Styrofoam.

One measure of people's interest in the generic-pronoun
problem was the response to a nationally syndicated article on
the subject by the columnist Tom Wicker, who reported that it
brought "the greatest single outpouring of mail" he had ever
received. Probably a better measure is the explosive increase in
alternatives to "generic" *he* in all media. More and more writers
and speakers seem to agree with the feeling expressed by psy-

chologist Wendy Martyna, who wrote, " 'He' deserves to live out its days doing what it has always done best—referring to 'he' and not 'she.' "

SOLVING THE PROBLEM

They as a Singular

> I corrected a boy for writing "no one . . . they" instead of "no one . . . he," explaining that "no one" was singular. But he said, "How do you know it was a he?"
>
> —A teacher

Children can be very logical. Although to some educated adults using *they* as a singular pronoun is like committing a crime, youngsters use it freely until someone convinces them they shouldn't. Most people, when writing and speaking informally, also rely on singular *they* as a matter of course, and so have many noted writers:

> "Every person . . . now recovered their liberty."
>
> —Oliver Goldsmith

> "Nobody prevents you, do they?"
>
> —William Makepeace Thackeray

> "I shouldn't like to punish anyone, even if they'd done me wrong."
>
> —George Eliot

> ". . . everyone shall delight us, and we them."
>
> —Walt Whitman

> ". . . everyone involuntarily looked at each other, and drew their breath."
>
> —Harriet Beecher Stowe

"Now, nobody does anything well that they cannot help doing."

—John Ruskin

"It's enough to drive anyone out of their senses."
—George Bernard Shaw

"[H]e did not believe it rested anybody to lie with their head high. . . ."

—Elizabeth Bowen

"You do not have to understand someone in order to love them."

—Lawrence Durrell

"And how easy the way a man or woman would come in here, glance around, find smiles and pleasant looks waiting for them, then wave and sit down by themselves."

—Doris Lessing

Everyday examples abound:

"Anyone using the beach after 5 P.M. does so at their own risk."

"Give someone a phone of their own."

"Disarm a drunk. Don't let them drive."

Once upon a time you *was a plural pronoun only. It assumed its singular function (replacing* thou) *in the days before prescriptive grammarians were around to inhibit that kind of change. English needs a comparable third person singular pronoun and, for many,* they *meets the need:*

"If you have a friend or relative who smokes too many cigarettes, sit them down in front of the television tonight to watch one of the most powerful anti-smoking programs ever made."

—Marc Gunther, TV review
The Hartford Courant

"If anyone doubts that democracy is alive and well, let them come to New Hampshire."
—Ronald Reagan

"You must identify the person who has the power to hire you and show them how your skills can help them with their problems."
—Richard Nelson Bolles
What Color Is Your Parachute?

"Each sailor who reads this book will be able to say honestly that they do finally know and understand the rules completely."
—Dave Perry, *Understanding the Yacht Racing Rules Through 1988*

The last two examples are representative of the ways pronouns are used throughout both of those popular reference manuals. The authors explain that they made a reasoned choice to use *they* as a singular indefinite pronoun, and that they use it consistently. When chided to "clean up" his grammar as a result of that choice, Richard Bolles' response is simple: "I have cleaned it up; my usage is quite deliberate."

Those who cannot bring themselves to use *they* in place of *he* sometimes produce sentences like:

"Nevertheless, everyone, the fastidious queen included, resigned himself sooner or later."

In another example, an article reporting that "Eudora Welty and Robert Penn Warren were featured luminaries of a Forum on Southern Writing" went on to say that

"Each author also presented an evening of readings from his own works."

In the first case, where the import of *everyone* is clearly plural, the phrase "resigned themselves" would be less jarring. In the second, "their own works" would convey equal billing more smoothly and at the same time avoid the gaffe of misrepresenting Welty's sex.

In still another instance a well-known author wrote:

> "[A] man or woman must learn to feel an emotional
> response before he is ready to undertake the
> dreadfully difficult problem of giving his love, his
> heart, to a being of the human kind."

Although the sexually inclusive image would have been sustained if the sentence had read

> [A] man or woman must learn to feel an emotional
> response before they are ready to undertake the
> dreadfully difficult problem of giving their love. . . .

perhaps the smell of chalk dust was so inhibiting to this writer that recasting the sentence from scratch was his only alternative.

He or She

Despite the charge of clumsiness, double-pronoun constructions have made a comeback, apparently on the reasonable grounds that words should reflect reality, as in the following:

> "If, however, that same trucker picks up a cargo at the
> Heinz plant to avoid returning home empty, he or she
> might well be in a pickle."
> —*New York Times* editorial

> "But the average American—exercising caution,
> weighing the risks, never investing more than he or
> she can afford to lose—can at least hope to keep even,
> and perhaps a step or two ahead of inflation."
> —James Daniel, *Reader's Digest*

> "To be black in this country is simply too pervasive an
> experience for any writer to omit from her or his work.
> It *has* to be there in one form or another."
> —Samuel R. Delany, *The Crisis*

(In connection with Delany's unaccustomed order, see **Order,** page 116; for abbreviated forms of *he or she,* see **Further Alternatives,** page 54.)

Pluralizing

The trouble with the *he or she* form is that it becomes awkward when repeated, as anyone trying to use the double-pronoun construction in an extended context soon discovers. In order to avoid that pitfall, a writer can often recast the material in the plural. The annually published catalog of a medical school, for example, formerly described the course of study undertaken by "the medical student" (who was always referred to as "he") in this way:

> "During his fourth-year studies . . . he assumes
> responsibilities in keeping with his stage of learning."

Nursing school catalogs of the same period invariably phrased curriculum descriptions in terms like

> As she gains experience and knowledge, the student
> nurse has increasing opportunities for clinical work.

When the materials are rewritten in the plural, the exclusive pronouns vanish, with the added advantage that the change both recognizes and encourages the growing numbers of women in medicine and men in nursing:

> "During their fourth-year studies . . . they assume
> responsibilities in keeping with their stage of learning."

> As they gain experience and knowledge, student
> nurses have increasing opportunities for clinical work.

Eliminating Pronouns

In describing the literary achievement of Sarah Orne Jewett, the critic F. O. Matthiessen wrote:

> "Style means that the author has fused his material and
> his technique with the distinctive quality of his
> personality."

Matthiessen's biographer, Giles B. Gunn, repeated his subject's evaluation of Jewett but in doing so eliminated the incongruous pronouns. "Style," Gunn wrote, is the

> "fusion of both technique and material with the distinctive qualities of a writer's own personality."

When it is important to focus on a nonspecific individual who might be of either sex, the same device often works. Instead of

> "A handicapped child may be able to feed and dress himself,"

the sentence could read

> A handicapped child may be able to eat and get dressed without help.

A social service agency's annual report used masculine-gender terms in explaining a legal decision that affected its work with clients. In the agency's words, the court ruled that

> "Information provided by a client to a social service agency is privileged in the same way as are communications between a lawyer and his client, a physician and his patient, or a clergyman and a penitent."

The sentence could have referred to

> communications between lawyer and client, physician and patient, or a member of the clergy and a penitent.

In other descriptions of one-to-one relationships, replacing pronouns with nouns and articles allows for the inclusion of both sexes. In the following example, the writer made it clear that a child's psychological parent may be either male or female but failed to make equally clear that the child may also be of either sex:

> "[A] child's relationship with a psychological parent, whether or not he or she is the child's natural parent, should never be interrupted. What counts in such a relationship is the child's degree of attachment and whether he feels wanted and needed—needed for himself, not for some financial advantage. . . ."

A possible revision:

[A] child's relationship with a psychological parent,
whether or not he or she is the child's natural parent,
should never be interrupted. What counts in such a
relationship is the child's degree of attachment and
feeling of being wanted and needed—needed as a
person, not for some financial advantage. . . .

Pronouns may also be eliminated by the device of repeating
the noun they refer to, even in examples that appear to present
insurmountable obstacles:

"Another cause of obscurity is that the writer is himself
not quite sure of his meaning. He has a vague
impression of what he wants to say, but has not, either
from lack of mental power or from laziness, exactly
formulated it in his mind, and it is natural enough that
he should not find a precise expression for a confused
idea."

E. B. White, in the third edition of *The Elements of Style,* used
that quotation from Somerset Maugham as an example of the
use of *he* as a "pronoun for nouns embracing both genders,"
which White called "a simple, practical convention rooted in the
beginnings of the English language." (See **Historical Background,** page 44.) He then revised the paragraph to illustrate
the "nonsense" that results when *he or she* is used "to affirm
equality of the sexes."

"Another cause of obscurity is that the writer is herself
or himself not quite sure of her or his meaning. He or
she has a vague impression . . ."

and so forth. Nonsense, of course, but the passage could have
been rewritten without pronouns and with one repetition of the
noun:

Another cause of obscurity is that the writer has a
vague impression of wanting to say something but has
not, either from lack of mental power or from laziness,
exactly formulated it mentally, and it is natural enough

that such a writer should not find a precise expression
for a confused idea.

As often happens in recasting a thought, redundancy is also
eliminated.

Sometimes the puzzle is not how to avoid using "generic"
pronouns, but how and why one ever crept into a sentence to
start with:

> "One hundred and twenty . . . college women were
> asked to evaluate eight paintings on the basis of the
> artist's technical competence, his creativity, overall
> quality and content of the painting, emotion expressed,
> and estimation of the artist's future success."

In such a case the rhythm as well as the sense are improved
when *his* is simply deleted.

Further Alternatives

Writing designed to give instructions or practical advice can
avoid the third-person pronoun problem by addressing the
reader directly. The financial columnist Sylvia Porter often uses
this form. For example:

> "The warehouse store is another way for you to curb
> your soaring food bills. . . . You, the customer, do your
> own bagging and loading of groceries into your car."

Porter also uses abbreviated double-pronoun constructions, as
in

> "After a victim of a consumer fraud discovers he/she
> has been ripped off . . ."

Legal contracts and other forms may be printed with *he/she, his/
her,* etc., so the inapplicable pronouns can be crossed out. Some
writers even favor a further abbreviation of the double-pronoun
construction:

> "Any amateur psychiatrist would be more sophisticated
> in the use s/he made of such 'data.' "

One sometimes serves as a third-person pronoun:

> A visitor to the island can spend as little as ten dollars a
> day provided he is willing to give up eating

can be recast to read

> When visiting the island, one can spend as little as ten
> dollars a day provided one is willing to give up eating.

It is a convenient pronoun to use of animals (see **The Ubiq-
uitous Male Animal** below), and at times is the obvious choice
when speaking of children:

> "To society, a baby's sex is second in importance only
> to its health."

> When the new baby comes, it's going to sleep in Lil's
> room.

> A wise child knows its own telephone number.

Some writers—Judith Martin among them—even use *it* of a
specific child, and with considerable humor:

> "Miss Manners once demanded of a six-year-old
> person how it could be so childish and was forced to
> admit the justice of its reply, 'I'm a child.' "

THE UBIQUITOUS MALE ANIMAL

> "Shrike: He often hunts when he isn't hungry—but he
> doesn't waste the extra food. . . ."

> "Dolphin: Probably the most intelligent mammal after
> man, this friendly and talkative creature has a built-in
> sonar system of his own."

These descriptions are from a mailing piece advertising an educational game for children, but the compulsion to refer to
animals in masculine-gender terms is not limited to advertising
copywriters. Even teachers and scientists fall into the habit of
using masculine pronouns for all creatures not specifically identified as female. When an adult sees a hawk riding a thermal

updraft and says to a child, "Look at him soar!" the child not only learns something about how hawks fly but also that all hawks are male and, by implication, that maleness is the norm.

In a review of a book about dinosaurs written for young children, the critic lamented the dearth of factual information provided and then said:

> "We learn just two things about Stegosaurus, for instance, that he had sharp, bony plates sticking up along his back and tail and that he ate plants."

It seems reasonable to expect, as well, that the fact-conscious reviewer not obscure the fact of Stegosaurus's sexual differentiation.

Using *it* is not offensive to animals and provides a simple way to avoid giving misinformation when generalizing or when the sex of an individual is unknown. The actual game cards referred to in the advertising copy at the beginning of this section used *it* consistently and naturally:

> "Each night the gorilla puts together a kind of bed, made of leaves, on which it sleeps through the night. It lives mainly on the ground. . . ."

> "The black rhinoceros is the only member of the genus *Diceros*. Like its cousin the white rhinoceros it bears two horns. . . ."

Oddly enough, some writers continue to use *it* even when the sex of the animal is germane. For example, an article about game cocks used *it* throughout, although cocks are by definition male. A science brief on bees, which began

> "When a foraging bee finds a particularly juicy clump of flowers, how does it relate that information to other bees in the hive?"

then went on to explain the

> " 'waggle dance,' a series of movements in which the female bee swings her abdomen and uses her wing musculature to produce a sound."

Such a switch in midstream is not as misleading as the practice of using *he* "generically," but it is confusing. One gathers, correctly, that foraging bees who do the "waggle dance" are always female, but the *it* in the first sentence leaves open the possibility that some nondancing foragers are male.

Sometimes a writer uses a gendered pronoun to avoid confusion with another *it* in the same sentence, as in

> "A groundhog's 'day' means more to us than it does to him."

The sentence might be recast to read

> A groundhog's "day" means more to us than to it (*or* means more to us than it does to the groundhog).

Reporters could not make up their minds what to call a great white shark that finally got away after being harpooned off Montauk Point a few years back. Marina operators, skippers, and pilots who sighted the animal were quoted as calling it variously "he," "she," and "it." Since the shark escaped, its sex is still unknown. Nor did anyone know the sex of a 40-ton humpback whale that spent three weeks in the Sacramento River before being lured back to sea by recordings of other humpbacks. In that case, however, someone made things a lot easier for the media by naming the whale "Humphrey," after which most reporters called it "he." The whale might have been dubbed "Hanna" or "Hortense"—or a double-duty name like "Happy." But it wasn't, a point the press ignored until scientists, wondering why a whale would be attracted to warm inland waters, began to speculate that "Humphrey" might be pregnant.

A NEW GENERIC PRONOUN?

In the nineteenth century Charles Converse of Erie, Pennsylvania, proposed a new word to serve as a common-gender pronoun meaning "he or she." Converse's invention was *thon* (a contraction of *that one*) with *thon's* as the possessive, and it was carried in American dictionaries into the 1950s. It may not have been the first neologism proposed to solve the pronoun problem, and it was far from the last.

In recent years a growing conviction that English needs a new sex-inclusive singular pronoun has produced myriad suggestions, such as *co, E, tey,* and *hesh.* Some of the proposals have been used in published materials or have become part of the everyday speech of people living in egalitarian communities. In her novel *The Cook and the Carpenter* (1973), June Arnold adopted *na* as a sex-neutral pronoun, and Marge Piercy used *person,* and the shorter form *per,* in *Woman on the Edge of Time* (1976). The 1979 edition of the supervisor's guide *Managers Must Lead!* by Ray A. Killian, published by American Management Associations, uses *hir* as a common-gender pronoun throughout. Interest in a new pronoun is especially strong among a group of psychologists whose studies have confirmed the inadequacy of "generic" *he.* Several of them have run tests in an effort to assess the functionality of various coined words, including some of the ones mentioned above, as common-gender singular pronouns.

Clearly, the need inspires a quest that will not die, and proposals for new pronouns can be expected to keep popping up for years. Whether or not a neologism ever takes hold, the continued and increased use of singular *they* in writing as well as speech—and the restitution of the status it enjoyed before grammarians arbitrarily proscribed it—now seems inevitable.

Language . . . is the repository of our shared wisdom (or lack of it) about the sexes. It is also the main vehicle whereby this wisdom is disseminated throughout society, between generations and across cultures—to be interpreted and accepted, or challenged, debated, transformed and rejected. . . .

—Philip M. Smith, *Language, the Sexes and Society*

3

Generalizations

ASSIGNING GENDER TO GENDER-NEUTRAL TERMS

The typical young adult in the United States today is more self-directed, more able to make thoughtful choices and grasp unexpected opportunities, than was her mother in the 1960s.

Something wrong? Not if you sanction the generic use of gender-specific terms. By a narrow statistical margin the "typical young adult in the United States today" is more likely to be female than male. Nevertheless, most people are surprised and even confused by a generalization about "young adults" phrased in terms of women.

Why, then, is it common to find similar generalizations in which masculine gender is assigned to generic words? In an article called "The Psyche of the Entrepreneur," for example, the writer described entrepreneurs as "supremely confident businessmen" in whom "a small child [often lurks] who is striving to create . . . the world he craved in his childhood, . . . outrivaling even his father." But wait. The author says that four out of ten new businesses are started by women, and that women's motives for becoming entrepreneurs differ from men's, among them being "the need to work while raising children" and "lack of opportunity in large corporations." So why wasn't the article called "The Psyche of the Male Entrepreneur"?

What the author adduced from the "sparse data that exists on female entrepreneurs" is that "men and women seem to resemble each other most" in "the talents that lead to success" whereas "they may differ most in their psychological motives." Very interesting information. It would provide good material for an article called "The Psyche of the Entrepreneur." But that is not what this article—its title notwithstanding—is about. Disregarding the people who start 40 percent of all new businesses, the author continued, "The force that propels the entrepreneur into his solitary orbit is the craving for autonomy."

The assignment of gender to a generic word is usually less deliberate, as in this example, where *adult* is equated with *adult male:*

> "Another difference between the Mariners and many other [fife and drum] corps is that it is strictly an adult group. It does not take in either women or students who are still in high school."

What the author presumably meant was

> Another difference between the Mariners and many other corps is that it is limited to men (*or* to adult males).

In another case a Southern author, writing satirically about how the rest of the country views Southerners, asked,

> "Who are these people? What are they like? Do they have any pastimes besides fighting, hunting, drinking and writing novels? Do they really sleep with their sisters and bay at the moon?"

At least some Southern women fight, hunt, drink, and write novels, but since the writer was apparently thinking only of

Southern men, it would have been more accurate either to say so or, as an alternative, to even the score by providing a brace of equally ironic questions about women:

> Who are these people? What are they like? Do they
> have any pastimes besides fighting, hunting, drinking
> and writing novels? Do their men really sleep with
> their sisters and bay at the moon? Do their women
> wear crinolines and stash their whiskey behind the
> camellias?

Men, in particular, seem to forget that "the average person" and "the species" are not limited to one sex. A newspaper columnist writes of the almost limitless number of human activities an "average person" crams into the space of one year:

> "The average person finds it no problem at all to have
> three head colds, one sunburn, an attack of athlete's
> foot, 20 headaches, three hangovers and five temper
> tantrums with adolescent children, and still get in his
> 61 hours of shaving. . . ."

Another, who would like to do away with neckties, writes:

> "But what earthly purpose is served by tying a knot
> around your neck every day just so you can look like
> every other member of the species?"

And a book reviewer describes H. G. Wells's ability to

> "exert his magnetism on the small boy in all of us."

In such cases, solutions are not difficult: "the average person" could be "the average male"; "every other member of the species" could be "every other man"; and "the small boy in all of us" could be "the child in all of us." Or, if the writer really means "the average person," an alternative to the clause on shaving could be something like "and still get in their 61 hours in the shower." What is less easy is to convince writers prone to androcentrism of the need to guard against it.

In a factual account, unconscious exclusion of one sex or the other can actually distort the information being presented. Sometimes the results, though frustrating, are funny. A syndi-

cated newspaper story on the Abkhasian people of Soviet Georgia, many of whom live vigorous lives well past their hundredth
birthdays, included this description:

> "They appear strikingly fit, unusually erect from long
> years on horseback, short but lean. Most have their
> own teeth under flamboyant silver mustaches."

Since nowhere in the thousand-word story did the writer refer
specifically to women, the puzzled reader is left to wonder
whether the fabled Abkhasian longevity is characteristic of male
Abkhasians only. Or is one supposed to believe that both sexes
sport flamboyant silver mustaches?

Similar absurdities arise when writers unconsciously assign
gender to other proper nouns like *Americans* or *the French*.

> Our neighbors in the next railway compartment were
> two Norwegians and their wives

might be stated, just as accurately,

> Our neighbors in the next railway compartment were
> two Norwegians and their husbands

or, more concisely,

> Our neighbors . . . were two Norwegian couples (*or*
> four Norwegians).

What people lose sight of is that although words like *wife* and
husband are either feminine or masculine in gender, words like
Norwegian and *neighbor* are sex-inclusive. You can say "My
neighbor is an artist and his wife is an investment banker" or
"My neighbor is an investment banker and her husband is an
artist," and which choice you make depends on your point of
view. Although it is disheartening that neutral terms are so
often automatically assigned to males, the example also illustrates a very positive change, for outside of fantasy no one, until
recently, would have referred to a woman in investment banking at all—however they might have phrased it. Women have
been neighbors for thousands of years, but they have been investment bankers for only a matter of decades.

The assignment of gender to common-gender nouns often has serious consequences, as when terms like *colonists, immigrants, slaves, settlers, pioneers,* and *farmers* are used in contexts that refer to males only:

> In the nineteenth century immigrants were met at the
> dock by party politicians who promised them jobs in
> exchange for their votes when they became citizens.

What the sentence really means, as we know from history, is

> In the nineteenth century immigrants were met at the
> dock by party politicians who promised jobs in
> exchange for the votes of the men when they became
> citizens.

Similarly,

> The Fifteenth Amendment was intended to insure the
> voting rights of former slaves

means

> The Fifteenth Amendment was intended to insure the
> voting rights of men who had been slaves.

The long-range effects of that kind of semantic carelessness are hard to assess, but immediate effects can be concrete and readily observed. A case in point involves the word *farmer.* Most farmers in the developing world are women. According to United Nations estimates, women produce 60 to 80 percent of the food supply in Africa and Asia. Until recently, however, these women were largely excluded from projects designed to help farmers in developing countries. As a former administrator of the United States Agency for International Development pointed out, "Western development experts simply assumed that farmers were male."

Closer to home, the Internal Revenue Service has been known to make the same assumption, as in the case of a woman who built up a sizable farm operation with her husband during their forty-three years of marriage. When her husband died, the IRS held that all the farm equipment had belonged to him and thus was included in his estate. But a federal district court ruled that the woman was equally responsible for the farm's success: she kept the books, marketed eggs, hauled cattle, cared for the hired hands, and helped harvest the grain. Declaring that it would not ignore

> "this farm wife's contribution to the success of the business,"

the court ordered the IRS to give her back some $40,000 of estate tax, plus interest. It seems clear, however, that if the IRS and the court had thought not in terms of "this farm wife's" contribution but rather of

> this farmer's contribution to the success of the business,

she would have been considered a full partner from the beginning, and the case might never have arisen.

The inability of many people to see women as farmers and farmers as women has led to belittling terms like *farmerette* and *farmeress*. (See **"Feminine" Suffixes,** page 134.) If a writer has reason to identify farmers by sex, *farm women* and *farm men* are useful parallel terms subsumed under the common-gender noun *farmer*.

LINGUISTIC ABUSE OF *WIVES*

> "The forces that keep the corporate wife in her place are powerful. . . ."

> "Once Senate wives rolled bandages for World War I wounded. Now they meet regularly to make nonpolitical talk along with hand puppets and clothing for a Washington children's hospital."

Terms like *corporate wives* and *Senate wives* reflect the continuing reality of male power preserves. Women thus identified as appendages both of a man and of an institution are usually expected to accept a well-defined role in support of the institution, and, in the case of the "corporate wife," to function in ways that in effect provide the corporation with two employees for the price of one. But since increasing numbers of women whose husbands hold high-level posts are pursuing careers of their own, terms like *Senate wives* and *corporate wives* have meaning only when they are used in such contexts as those quoted above.

> Senate wife Mary Able is a professor of biochemistry at XYZ University

is a misuse of *Senate wife*, for the point is not that Mary Able is married to a senator but that she teaches biochemistry. If Senator Able is to be mentioned at all, an alternative might be

> Mary Able, whose husband is Senator Harry Able, is . . .

or

> Mary Able is a professor of biochemistry at XYZ University. She and her husband, Senator Harry Able, . . .

Sometimes the irrelevant use of *wives* is deliberately pejorative. When a group of women in the Washington, D.C., area proposed rating rock-music recordings whose lyrics combine sex and violence, a magazine editorialized:

> ". . . the Washington Wives' activities can be seen as just another attempt to muzzle rock & roll. . . ."

In addition to its implication that the women proposed censoring the industry, the editorial use of *wives* served to discredit the women personally by suggesting they had attracted attention to their cause only because their husbands held important posts in the federal government.

Faculty wives, a familiar term a generation ago, has pretty much given way to *faculty spouses* at schools where women teach in more than token numbers. Similarly, *service wives* sounds increasingly dated as more women enter the military and other government services. In reporting the moment when Jimmy Carter embraced Leonid Brezhnev after signing the second strategic arms limitation treaty, *New York Times* correspondent Craig R. Whitney wrote:

> "The gesture evoked cheers and applause from the hundreds of diplomats, delegation members, their

> spouses and journalists who gathered for the historic signing."

Corporate wives and even *Senate wives* may also be traveling the road to obsolescence. (See **Women as Entities, Not Appendages,** page 108.)

Fortunately the mention of wives sometimes performs an unexpected but valuable linguistic service: it blows the whistle on a writer who is unconsciously assigning masculine gender to a generic word. Here are a few examples:

> "The American adult goes into a world that does not 'owe him a living' . . . and the only person he will be able to trust when he gets out there will be his little wife. . . ."

> "I suppose any normal American would rather sit with his wife in a public place than apart from her. . . ."

> "There's no real commonality among programmers. I don't know that we beat our wives any more than anyone else."

> "It's the great secret of doctors, known only to their wives . . . that most things get better by themselves. . . ."

And a book about "America's sexual revolution" is titled

> *Thy Neighbor's Wife.*

GRATUITOUS MODIFIERS

As Putdowns

> "Powerful lady attorney and confident young lawyer team up to defend a wealthy contractor accused of murder."
>
> —TV listing

Question: What sex are the confident young lawyer and the wealthy contractor?

If for some reason identifying the sex of the protagonists in this television show about lawyers was important, why didn't the listing read

> Powerful attorney and her young male colleague team
> up to defend a wealthy businessman accused of
> murder.

The answer is that in our culture we are not inclined to diminish a man's prestige. Nor should we be. But that is what labeling someone with an incidental characteristic like sex or color or national origin does. In real life, competence depends on things like training, experience, talent, and personality, and these are qualities the words *powerful* and *confident* suggest. Using a gratuitous modifier like *lady* to shift attention from what is genuinely relevant to what will titillate television viewers may be an accepted ploy in the ratings game. But even so, should it always be done at the expense of women?

Sometimes, as in the television example, gratuitous modifiers are used purposely. More often they slip in as a result of prejudice or out of habit.

> "But I got a contrary reaction from a woman attorney I
> talked to who is an expert in the field. . . . 'You are
> doing a foolhardy thing,' she said."

could have been

> But I got a contrary reaction from another attorney I
> talked to who is an expert in the field. . . .

Since the reader will discover from the feminine-gender pronoun the incidental fact that the expert referred to is a woman, the qualifier was as superfluous as the interpolated words *a man* would have been in another sentence from the same account:

> "I rushed to the pay phone in the hall and started
> phoning lawyers I knew until I found one, *a man,* who
> was in his office."

In activities or professional fields where men are outnumbered by women, they are the ones who get the gratuitous modifiers, and with the same result:

> Walt Whitman was a male nurse during the Civil War

could have been

> Walt Whitman was a nurse during the Civil War.

As with women, such a sex qualifier is usually unnecessary. Its suggestion that "male nurses," "male secretaries," or "male kindergarten teachers" are not *real* nurses, secretaries, or kindergarten teachers is demeaning, and the implication that people who hold those jobs are always female is no more true today than the assumption that all lawyers, doctors, and engineers are male. The following example illustrates the basic message conveyed, which is that whatever is identified by a superfluous sex qualifier is a deviation from the standard:

> "This formidable five-eyed female may eat her mate
> for dinner. . . . She's the female praying mantis."

Is a female praying mantis not a true member of her species? If one grants that she is, why not let the pronouns indicate her sex?

> This formidable five-eyed creature may eat her mate
> for dinner. . . . She's the praying mantis.

Were the dining proclivities of female and male praying mantises reversed, would anyone be likely to add the redundant adjective *male*?

> This formidable five-eyed male may eat his mate for
> dinner. . . . He's the male praying mantis.

Those tempted to say yes may be surprised that lexicographers do not necessarily agree. After describing bowerbirds in terms of taxonomy and location, Webster's Second Unabridged Dictionary continues,

> "They build *bowers* or *runs* . . . which are used as
> playhouses and to attract the females. . . .

The wording in early editions of Webster's Third also implies by omission that the male bowerbird is the standard:

"any of a group of . . . passerine birds . . . of the
Australian region that build chambers or passages . . .
used as playhouses or to attract the females. . . ."

Not until the 1974 Collegiate did the Merriam-Webster editors
admit females to full bowerbirddom:

"any of various passerine birds . . . of the Australian
region in which the male builds a chamber or passage
. . . used esp. to attract the female."

This example is not an isolated one. A popular bird identification book, which has gone into at least fourteen printings,
provides photographs of "the cardinal" and "the ♀ cardinal,"
and several dictionaries define certain species of deer (e.g., the
fallow deer) with reference to their antlers without making clear
that antlers are characteristic of the male only.

Usage arbiters at the *New York Times* came to grips with the
implications of gratuitous modifiers after three items had appeared in the same column of news briefs mentioning, respectively, "women students," a "woman photographer," and a
"woman customer." An in-house bulletin from the news desk
commented: "The use of *woman* as a modifier suggests that such
words as *student, photographer* and *customer,* unadorned, are masculine. . . . [P]robably the time has come to banish *woman* as an
adjective; we don't use *man* that way. When a person's sex is
truly newsworthy, let us use the same kinds of construction for
both sexes: *male students, female students; lawyers who are women,
lawyers who are men."* ,

Unintentional Distortion

Gratuitous modifiers can also distort meaning. The author of
an article on Dunbar High School, the first public high school
for blacks in the United States, described one graduate of the
days when Dunbar was still segregated as

"the first black general in the United States Army"

and another as

"one of the nation's leading black historians."

In the first instance the adjective *black* was appropriate; in the second it was not. The author may have meant

one of the nation's leading authorities on black history

or

a black who is one of the nation's leading historians

or

a leader among the nation's historians who are black.

When, as above, the use of a modifier obscures the question of whether the person referred to is being judged on a par with everyone else or only within a limited category, it is particularly damaging. In an article on Alicia de Larrocha, the critic Donal Henahan said that to call her "the greatest woman pianist of our day . . . serves, like most labels, to discourage thought." It skirts the question, Henahan wrote, of whether de Larrocha "might actually be one of the finest living pianists. . . . [It] diminishes de Larrocha's achievements by ghettoizing them."

"Damn Good for a Woman"

The youngster who says, "I ate all my broccoli and didn't even say how much I hate it" is skilled at apophasis, which Webster's Second Unabridged defines as "mention of something in disclaiming intention to mention it." Apophasis can also be an effective, if somewhat underhanded, political device, as when a candidate says, "I do not intend to make an issue of my opponent's lavish personal expense account." But when speakers or writers try to use it to beat the gratuitous modifier, apophasis backfires:

"She is the kind of judge who no one would say is a 'woman judge'—she's a judge."

"No one will ever call her a 'lady anthropologist.' "

Such expressions suggest that women who excel professionally are double aberrations: as women ("She can't be a real professional") and as professionals ("She can't be a real woman").

She is an excellent judge

and

She is a first-rate anthropologist

are direct and free of the implication "Damn good for a woman." *The London Times Literary Supplement* offered a straightforward assessment based solely on relevant grounds when it called Muriel Spark

"the best English novelist writing today."

Relevance and Irrelevance

In some circumstances sex, like race, may be a significant part of the information to be conveyed:

"Margaret Thatcher won a governing majority today as Europe's first woman prime minister."

On October 2, 1967, Thurgood Marshall became the first black justice of the Supreme Court of the United States.

But this information need not be repeated endlessly. Once barriers have been breached and stereotypes dispelled, race and sex become irrelevant and intrusive factors, as in

Dr. John Adams, a prominent black pediatrician, has been named medical director of Children's Hospital. Other staff changes this month include the retirement of Dr. Paul Zenkel as chief of the Cardiac Service. He will be replaced by a woman, Dr. Harriet Mooney.

A nonracist, nonsexist version would read:

Dr. John Adams, a prominent pediatrician, has been named medical director of Children's Hospital. In other staff changes this month, Dr. Paul Zenkel retires as chief of the Cardiac Service, and Dr. Harriet Mooney becomes the new chief.

SPORTS REPORTING

The headline on a newspaper story about two track and field events, the Memorial Relays held in Teaneck, New Jersey, and the Nanuet Relays held in Nanuet, New York, reads:

"SCHOOLBOYS STRUGGLE
AGAINST CHILL, RAIN."

For six paragraphs the wording seems appropriate. Then comes a paragraph beginning:

"In the girls' competition at the Memorial Relays . . ."

The rest of the story deals only with boys' events; if girls competed at Nanuet, they were not mentioned.

This ho-hum approach to schoolgirl sports is common. The attitude of some reporters seems to be that girls (and women) don't count since they are rarely competitive with boys (and men), who do count. But that is like saying heavyweight bouts are the only real boxing contests when in fact the International Olympic Committee awards gold, silver, and bronze medals to men in twelve different classes, and at last count the World Boxing Association and the World Boxing Council both recognized thirteen championship divisions for men ranging from Flyweight to Heavyweight. It is this recognition of individual and class differences that sportswomen also merit.

Fortunately the last few years have brought a marked change in the amount of space allotted to women's contests, and—equally important—the language sportswriters use in describing women's events is becoming more evenhanded. Writers cannot completely counteract the putdown implicit in such nonparallel titles as the Professional Golfers' Association and the Ladies Professional Golfers' Association, or in the names bestowed on women's high school and college teams: the Lady Knights, the Lady Stags, the Grizzlyettes, the Lumberjills, and the Yellow Jackettes to name a few. (Some are even more trivializing: at a state college where the men's teams are called the Blue Hawks, the women's teams are called the Blue Chicks; and then there are the Presidents and the First Ladies, the Sea Gulls and the She Gulls.) At least administrators are occasionally being challenged on this score, however. When one university changed all its teams from the Redmen—in response to strong objections from Native Americans—to the Minutemen, a reporter who questioned the new choice was told by the Sports Information Director, "*Minutemen* is a generic term." But he went on to say, "If there are people who are sensitive, we use [the university's initials] in our press releases about women's teams. Ninety-nine percent of the time we try to avoid *Minutemen*."

Separate administrative divisions for men's teams and women's teams may also encourage the latter's recognition: men's swimming and women's swimming, men's crew and women's crew, women's and men's archery, handball, alpine skiing, gymnastics, and so forth. That is the Olympic tradition, and it has been accepted by a growing number of schools and colleges. A college magazine, for example, reports:

> "The men's hockey program . . . has experienced a
> notable revival of spirit and support in the past two
> seasons. . . ."
>
> "The women's swim team opened its season with a
> road victory over. . . ."

Another college, which used the picture of a women's soccer team on the cover of its Fall Sports Schedule, lists men's teams and women's teams as such when it fields both, but calls its teams in single-sex sports "Varsity Field Hockey" and "Varsity Football."

This kind of parallel treatment does not deny that in intercollegiate sports some men's competitions result in a bigger gate than all women's contests put together, but it acknowledges that unless the sole purpose of college athletics is to make money, women deserve more than token recognition.

The same is true at the high school level, where the kind of writing represented by the first example that follows is gradually giving way to that of the second, and in the process building interest in long-neglected girls' contests.

> Oakville High's basketball team will play Smithtown this Thursday, and the girls' basketball team will meet Smithtown's girls on Friday. Varsity coach Al Heinz said, "We have what it takes, and we're about to prove it. . . ." Since Thursday's game is the last one before the divisional playoffs, Oakville fans hope Heinz knows what he's talking about.

> Oakville High's varsity basketball teams will meet Smithtown this week, the boys Thursday and the girls Friday. Al Heinz, the boys' coach, said, "We have what it takes, and we're about to prove it. . . ." Oakville girls' coach Sally Rubin wasn't pulling a long face either. . . .

In reporting women's and girls' athletics it is no more necessary to mention the players' sex in the headline and in every other paragraph than it is to refer to the sex of male players. Since feminine-gender pronouns and the players' names speak for themselves, repeated reference to "the girls," "Oakville's girl players," or "these talented young women" slows the pace and distracts the reader.

So do social titles, though fortunately very few style manuals still insist on the use of such titles when a women's match is being reported. The suggestion of barbed repartee over teacups that colored this account,

> "Finding pinpoint accuracy with her swift rival at net, Mrs. Lloyd continued to send shots whizzing past Miss Navratilova, finally evening the score at 5–5. Miss Navratilova hit two sizzling overheads . . ."

has given way to the description of a genuine contest:

> "Leading by 3–1, and serving a deuce in the first set, Navratilova hit a half-volley. . . ."

First-rate sports reporting, whether of a major-league baseball game or a high school soccer match, concentrates on the game and the players, not on their sex or marital situation.

In sports writing, as in other fields, gratuitous modifiers can also distort meaning. When Nancy Lopez was a rookie, she won more money than any other rookie golfer, male or female.

> Nancy Lopez is an outstanding woman golfer who held
> the rookie winnings record her first year on the circuit

implies that Lopez held the record for women. She did, of course, but since she also held the overall record,

> Nancy Lopez is an outstanding golfer who made more
> money her first year on the circuit than any other
> rookie golfer of either sex

makes her achievement clear.

PERSONIFICATION

Signs of the times:

> In a *Ladies Home Journal* cartoon by Henry Martin, a
> woman in a convertible pulls up to a gas pump and
> says to the attendant "Fill him up!"

> The National Weather Service has altered its twenty-
> five-year practice of identifying all hurricanes by
> women's first names. Every other one now blows in as
> the namesake of a man. It's Anna, Bob, Claudette,
> David, etc.

> When the United States Navy was reported to be
> considering whether to stop calling its ships "she," a
> Bill Kitchen cartoon accompanying the news report
> showed a pair of male sailors in a bar clutching their
> beer steins as one anxiously queries the other:
> "Where's it all going to end, Simpson? Where's it all
> going to end?"

The question some people might be tempted to ask first is, where did it all begin? Neither Simpson nor anyone else knows the answer, of course, for personification began long before recorded history. Among the earliest artifacts known to archae-ologists are human representations, assumed to be of deities, indicating that for millennia God was personified as female. Today most religions, while insisting that God has no sex, rely heavily on male symbols for the Godhead (including the linguistic symbols *Father* and *He*), reserving female ones for subordinate entities like the Church.

This patriarchal religious tradition strongly influenced the development of the English language and the outlook of its speakers. In 1646 J. Poole, a grammarian, explained that "The Masculine is more worthy than the Feminine, and the Feminine is more worthy than the Neuter," and in 1795 another grammarian, L. Murray, had this to say of personification:

> Figuratively, in the English tongue, we commonly give the masculine gender to nouns which are conspicuous for the attributes of imparting or communicating, and which are by nature strong and efficacious. Those, again, are made feminine which are conspicuous for the attributes of containing or bringing forth, or which are peculiarly beautiful or amiable. Upon these principles the sun is always masculine, and the moon, because the receptacle of the sun's light, is feminine. The earth is generally feminine. A ship, a country, a city, &c. are likewise made feminine, being receivers or containers. Time is always masculine, on account of its mighty efficacy. Virtue is feminine from its beauty, and its being the object of love. Fortune and the church are generally put in the feminine gender. . . .

Today, personification is applied to fewer things and, as Simpson's friend was aware, the stereotypes it once sought to enshrine no longer go unchallenged.

A newspaper account of the Coast Guard icebreaker-tug *Katmai Bay*, which operates on Lake Superior, consistently referred to the ship as "she." The ship's skipper, however, was quoted as follows:

> "Working side by side, two of these ships could handle any ice the Great Lakes can dish up. If one gets stuck, it backs up while the other charges ahead. Then it in turn charges."

In a television science program on the wreck of the *Amoco Cadiz*, a disaster that resulted in a massive oil spill along the coast of Brittany in 1978, the narrator sometimes referred to the doomed tanker as "it," sometimes as "she." In describing the wreck itself, however, he used imagery that was both anthropomorphic and female:

> "Less than a mile offshore, the *Amoco Cadiz* was steadily hemorrhaging into the sea. . . . Fourteen hours later, the ship impaled herself on the rocks."

Disasters are frequently personified as female. Public pressure was responsible for the National Weather Service decision to divvy up "responsibility" for the devastation caused by hurricanes, and the significance of the switch became clear as soon as hurricanes Bob, David, Fred, and Henri hit the headlines. Not only did newscasters and weather reporters show reluctance to personify them in negative imagery, but as the *NOW National Times* commented: "After the early 'him-icane' jokes . . . wore off, most radio and television weather forecasters made 'Bob' a genderless 'it' in record time. It was nothing like the old days when hurricanes with female names were known to 'flirt with the Florida coast,' were 'perfectly formed,' had tempers that 'teased and threatened.' "

But "Mother Nature" still gets "her" lumps. An ad for a rustproofing compound for automobiles shows the picture of a vicious-looking woman with long, blood-red fingernails, and the copy reads:

> "Don't let Mother Nature rip you off! She's out to kill your car's new finish. . . . Stop her. . . ."

Nuclear power plants are also female by implication. The accident at the Three Mile Island plant in Pennsylvania led to discussion of conditions at that facility's "sister" (never "brother") plants across the country. Similarly the product of an element's radioactive decay is known as the element's "daughter."

In English the personification of objects and ideas has more rhetorical impact than in languages where every noun has grammatical gender. A German translation of the woman saying to the gas station attendant "Fill him up!" wouldn't even get a chuckle in Bonn because *Kraftwagen,* the German word for *automobile,* is a masculine-gender noun and takes a masculine pronoun as a matter of course. The French word *navire,* meaninig "ship," is also masculine, so a ship is referred to as "he" *(il)* in France, as are a parsnip, a refrigerator, and a flowerpot—all without sexual connotation.

The other notable aspect of personification in English is that many more things are represented as female than male. Just as men have influenced our language more than women have, so their fantasies have more often assigned characteristics of the "other" sex to nonliving things. When personified at all, virtuous concepts like justice and liberty are still (gallantly) accorded femaleness, whereas all-powerful forces like time and death are still male. Centers of action, the sun and the mind, are still stereotypically male; their more passive counterparts, the moon and the soul, still female. Except in art and poetry, however, entities like justice, time, the soul, and the sun are rarely represented as though they have sexual attributes. In everyday English, the largest category where personification persists is that of vehicles and mechanized contraptions, all of which are sometimes called "she."

It is easy to argue that

> She's the most beautiful boat in the harbor

or

> She sails like a bird

imply compliments to women, but the sexual association is less flattering when someone refers to a cranky piece of equipment as a "bitch" or advises a friend trying to start an old motor to

> Give her a kick and she'll turn over.

"Herman," a mechanized device used at nuclear installations to perform tasks that would expose human beings to intolerable levels of radiation, is an exception to the "machines are female" assumption. Perhaps the tradition that the mind is male still predominates—even when the "mind" is a robot's.

Personifications, like other arbitrary classifications, grow out of cultural preconceptions. A few are innocuous, some destructive, but all, in common with other forms of stereotyping, can work to discourage fresh perceptions. Writers who use it to identify something inanimate are not tempted to rely on supposedly universal sex-linked characteristics to make their point. Instead, they must find precise words to delineate the thing itself.

[W]e pay for our propensity to categorize. Once categorized, entities tend to be judged and evaluated on the basis of their category membership, to the neglect of their individual attributes. Sensitivity to differences among individuals within categories may be reduced, while sensitivity to differences between categories is accentuated.

—Philip M. Smith, *Language, the Sexes and Society*

4

Seeing Women and Girls as People

MASCULINITY, FEMININITY, AND OTHER SEX-LINKED DESCRIPTIVES

The characteristics we habitually identify as "womanly" and "feminine"—receptivity, tenderness, and nurturance, to name a few of the positive ones—can also characterize men. And contrary to conventional wisdom, women share such "manly" and "masculine" attributes as boldness, vigor, directness, and courage. These adjectives and their associates, terms like *masculinity* and *femininity, manliness* and *womanliness,* have become so overlaid with societal dogmas setting forth what women and men "should" be like that they have lost almost all meaning. Whose "should" are we talking about, and how do we know from one use to the next what subjective cast these sex-linked words are intended to convey?

What was meant, for example, when one important federal official said of another,

> "She seems to be able to blend a high professional
> standing and ability with an undeniable femininity.
> And she is also as tough as nails."

Was the speaker using *femininity* to mean "tenderness" or "nurturance"? Judging by the second sentence, it would appear he was not. Since "seems to be able to blend" implies a potential discrepancy between "femininity" and "high professional standing and ability," perhaps his intended meaning was something like

> She seems to be able to blend a high professional
> standing and ability with modest self-effacement . . . (*or*
> undeniable coquettishness . . . *or* an air of helpless
> fragility).

But those images do not go with "tough as nails" either. If the speaker meant he found his colleague appealing sexually, he might have phrased his comment

> She seems to be able to blend a high professional
> standing and ability with undeniable sex appeal.

Whatever the speaker's intention, the silliness of *femininity* in this context becomes obvious when a male subject is substituted:

> He seems to be able to blend a high professional
> standing and ability with an undeniable masculinity.

A phrase frequently heard in the 1980s,

> "the feminization of poverty,"

presents even more complex problems. Since poverty can hardly be characterized as tender, nurturing, or sexy, does the expression mean "making poverty appropriate for women," which the compound suffix, in its sense of "action or process," implies? The editor Donna Allen points out that the "feminization of anything is a GOOD thing, and it's not possible to make poverty good even by feminizing it." A more accurate phrase to describe the consequences of shredding the safety net, in the words of the writer Paula Kassell, is simply

"the pauperization of women."

A little comparative checking in current dictionaries shows that we tend to use words like *manly* and *masculine* to connote human qualities most people aspire to, qualities like bravery and strength of character. In the definitions of these masculine-gender words, few if any negative attributes are mentioned. In contrast, words like *womanly* and *feminine* connote qualities assigned to women as women. In addition to positive ones like tenderness and receptivity, the definers frequently imply that what typically makes someone "womanly" are many not-so-admirable characteristics, among them weakness, petulance, timidity, and fickleness. Women, it is true, are often weak, petulant, timid, and fickle. But what is concealed in our lexicon of sex-linked adjectives is that men are too. In short, women are linguistically saddled with their human failings, men are linguistically disassociated from theirs.

One result of this dichotomy is that English lacks active, strong words to use specifically of women. If the sentence

Assemblywoman Gray's campaign was notable for her womanly response to her critics

means

Assemblywoman Gray's campaign was notable for her gracious response to her critics,

it would be well to use the specific word *gracious*, for *womanly* might be interpreted as equivalent to a number of other terms frequently used of women in politics: *abrasive, emotional,* and *strident* among them.

Nor would one speak of

Golda Meir's womanful determination to carry on despite her illness

in the same way one might speak of

John Wayne's manful fight against cancer.

Yet those two human beings shared a brand of courage and
determination the word *manful* brings to mind as no comparable
feminine-gender term succeeds in doing.

Recently at least one of the feminine-gender adjectives has
been showing signs of acquiring new connotations of inner
strength and resourcefulness. The phrase

"the womanly art of directing turbines"

appeared in an advertisement featuring an electrical engineer
who is a woman. Although the copywriter's intent is not crystal
clear, at least the use of *womanly* in this context adds a welcome
dimension to one current dictionary's definition, which notes
that the word implies resemblance to a woman "in appropriate,
fitting ways" and gives as examples "womanly decorum, mod-
esty."

Hagar the Horrible

When a governor, seeking support for his tax proposals, asked legislators to

> "be manly enough or womanly enough to stand up and vote for these taxes"

he also used *womanly* in a still-novel way. He might have conveyed his meaning more succinctly by asking the legislators to

> be courageous enough to stand up and vote for these taxes.

Or it may be that his inclusion of women was an afterthought. If so, he managed in one breath to get his foot out of his mouth and, by attaching to *womanly* the qualities now defined under *manly*, to give women their just due.

On the whole, as these examples show, sex-linked adjectives are not very useful in describing the human traits and qualities both sexes share: they are too elusive and subjective to be precise, and they arrogate to one sex attributes both possess. Although it is sometimes hard to pick words that exactly convey the meaning intended, making the effort almost always guarantees clearer writing.

GIRLS, LADIES, FEMALES, WOMEN

It sometimes takes a well-attuned ear to make appropriate choices from among the everyday words used for female human beings. One problem is that all these words have psychic overtones: of immaturity and dependence in the case of *girl;* of decorum and conformity in the case of *lady;* of sexuality and reproduction in the case of both *female* and *woman*. (See **Reference Notes,** page 171.) But all have been invested with other meanings as well, both positive and negative, and no one knows for sure which way any one of them is moving—into the mainstream or out. The following observations, then, are primarily intended to provide perspective. In this area, perhaps more than in any other, the question to ask in making choices is whether the comparable masculine-gender term would or would not be appropriate.

Girl and *Gal*

What separates the women from the girls—linguistically as well as biologically—is age. A person may appropriately be called a "girl" until her middle or late teens. After that, although her family and close friends may go on calling her a girl with impunity, most red-blooded women find the term offensive. Just as *boy* can be blatantly offensive to minority men, arousing feelings of helplessness and rage, so *girl* can have comparable patronizing and demeaning implications for women.

The young police officer who calls out "Good morning, girls" to two middle-aged women may intend no insult, but his greeting is an affront just the same: one adult has treated two other adults as children, and they have no adequate riposte. Similarly business executives who make pompous statements like

I'll have my girl run off some copies right away

are enhancing their own self-image at the expense of someone else's.

I'll ask my secretary (*or* assistant *or* Ms. Blake) to run off some copies right away

conveys respect and recognition. Women in full-time office jobs may be assistants, clerks, secretaries, executives, bookkeepers, managers, etc., but unless their employers are violating the child labor laws, they are rarely girls.

How strongly women feel about being called "girls" was indicated when United Technologies, as part of a corporate-image series, took a full-page advertisement in the *Wall Street Journal* headed "Let's Get Rid of 'The Girl.'" Other ads in the same series drew numerous requests for reprints, but the ad that ended, "'The girl' is certainly a woman when she's out of her teens. Like you, she has a name. Use it." brought the greatest response of all, including congratulatory telephone calls, telegrams, and even flowers.

College and university women are not girls either, and today the "career girl" is as rare a bird as the "career boy." A brochure advertising

Ideal Luggage for the Career Girl

would almost certainly attract fewer buyers than would the claim

Ideal Luggage for the Business Woman

One accepted use of *boy* for an adult male occurs in the British term *old boy,* meaning a graduate of a preparatory school. This usage has been imported to the United States in *the old-boy network,* an expression that describes the exclusive, informal system —"old boysmanship"—long used by upper-class men to help their old school buddies into positions of power. Today the small but growing number of women in high-level corporate and government posts also constitute a network, and they are helping other women onto the job ladder and up the rungs. Thus, as in this *Washington Post* story, a new use of *girl* has become eminently appropriate:

" 'OLD-GIRL NETWORK'
HELPS WOMEN GAIN HIGH POSTS

In and around the time-honored 'old-boy network,'
which has tended to elude or exclude them, the 'girls'
are weaving their own web of firstname
acquaintanceships. . . ."

A variation of *girl,* often used by writers or speakers who sense that *girl* would be resented, is *gal.* Since *gal* is *girl* in disguise, using it is apt to be an out-of-the-frying-pan-into-the-fire solution. However, *gal* may possibly be useful in the kind of context that makes *guy* acceptable (a "guys and gals" sort of ambience), and it can sometimes serve well when deliberately chosen for its incongruity. For example, referring to an active ninety-year-old as "a feisty old gal" might be paying her a greater compliment than "feisty oldster" or "plucky senior citizen" would ever succeed in doing.

Lady

Lady is used most effectively to evoke a certain standard of propriety, correct behavior, or elegance. In Jennie Churchill's words,

"You may be a princess or the richest woman in the
world, but you cannot be more than a lady."

Because of these strong connotations, *lady* is not a synonym for
woman in the primary sense of that word any more than *gentleman* is a synonym for *man.*

A Phoenix lady has been named to the Liquor
Commission

is arch. A better choice would be

A Phoenix woman has been named . . .

or, using an appropriate identification,

A former president of the American Red Cross in
Phoenix has been named to the Liquor Commission.

However, *lady* can successfully suggest a certain éclat, as in

My grandmother smokes cigars like a lady.

Used informally in descriptive phrases, the noun can also imply
sophistication and gutsy determination:

"Katherine Hepburn is one terrific lady."

A headline writer at the *Los Angeles Times* managed to combine
the suggestion of éclat, sophistication, and gutsiness in

"MUGGER MEETS HIS MATCH
IN REAL LADY"

since the story itself, picked up from *The Guardian,* began

"When a 38-year-old member of New York's army of
muggers chose 87-year-old Lady Sarah Tucker of
England as his victim, he didn't know what he was
getting into"

and ended—after Lady Tucker had bashed her attacker over
the head with her umbrella, and a truck driver and police officer
had come to her assistance—

"Lady Tucker refused the police officer's offer of
medical aid but accepted his arm and allowed him to
escort her to her home."

Honorary epithets like *first lady* and *leading lady* also reflect esteem, but when incorporated in a job title, *lady* usually implies a lesser valuation. One never hears a congresswoman referred to as a "congresslady," and *cleaning lady* or *forelady* convey a condescension lacking in the more forthright *cleaning woman, cleaner, forewoman,* and *supervisor.* Similarly a woman in real estate who handles the sale of a $20-million office building is more likely to be called a "saleswoman," "sales agent," or "sales representative" than a "saleslady."

Like other unnecessary words, *lady* has a diminishing effect when dragged in:

> Her colleagues know her as a fighting lady to be
> reckoned with

is stronger as

> Her colleagues know her as a fighter to be reckoned
> with.

When used as an adjective, *lady* often signals "this woman is not to be taken seriously" (see **Gratuitous Modifiers,** page 66). A television newscaster who reported

> "In Moscow a lady streetcleaner has been arrested for
> fraud. . . ."

was ostensibly telling a straight story about someone who failed to deliver after accepting money to find people apartments. If the newscaster had begun

> In Moscow, a streetcleaner has been arrested for
> fraud. . . .

and let pronouns indicate the streetcleaner's sex, he would have avoided giving the impression that he was ridiculing a woman because of her job—one, as it happens, many women hold in the Soviet Union. If the caveat seems strained, imagine a similar story about a "gentleman streetcleaner."

A mail-order catalog copywriter may have discouraged sales of one item by describing it as a

> "Ladies' Tool Kit."

The kit pictured contained a hammer, pliers, utility knife, five wrenches, and a screwdriver handle with six interchangeable blades—the kind of items anyone of either sex might find handy to have around the house. A more appropriate description would have been

Home Tool Kit

One catalog recipient who does her own home repairs said of the ad: "Calling it a 'ladies' tool kit' means to me the tools are probably more showy than useful." Her comment might apply equally to items labeled "ladies' fly rod," "ladies' typewriter," or "ladies' razor"—all of which, rightly or wrongly, inadvertently advertise themselves as flimsy versions of standard items.

Ladies will no doubt go on being used in consort with *gentlemen,* as in the traditional salutation of public speakers "Ladies and gentlemen. . . ." And although Americans seldom use either term to refer to family pedigree, they do use both *ladies* and *gentlemen* to acknowledge a self-image or, sometimes, to inculcate one. It is in this latter sense—and often in contexts related to personal grooming and attire—that phrases like "gentleman's aftershave lotion" or "lady's handbag" or "silk long johns for ladies and gentlemen" crop up in the copywriter's lexicon.

The image is skewed toward "Beauty and the Beast," however, when the tandem usage slips from "ladies and gentlemen" into "ladies and men," as happened in another mail-order catalog. A sales pitch for "distinctive towels and bathrobes [as seen in] Europe's finest luxury hotels and spas," went on to explain that

"The robes come in a kimono unisex style with one size for men and one for ladies."

As usual, the best test of the appropriateness of *ladies* is whether or not the parallel masculine-gender word sounds natural. In this instance

one size for men and one for women (*or* one size for gentlemen and one for ladies), would do, although neither solution solves the problem the catalog poses for those not-so-rare creatures, small gentlemen and large ladies.

In the adjective *ladylike* the positive associations of *lady* are usually obscured by negative ones. A reviewer of the published memoirs of Eleanor Roosevelt commented, for example, that the book's format

> "enables the reader to follow the growth of her
> personality and outlook, from ladylike clichés to
> statesmanlike judgments."

The difficulty here is not only the use of *ladylike* to mean "ineffectual" or "meaningless"; it is also the juxtaposition of a negative, female-associated word with a positive, male-associated one. An alternative might have been

> . . . from empty clichés to considered judgments

or

> . . . from stilted responses to authoritative opinions.

Female

Used either as a noun or an adjective, *female* is appropriate when the corresponding choice for the other sex would be *male:*

> Maggie had her puppies last night, three females and
> two males

sounds natural, whereas

> The Festival String Quintet includes two females

does not. On the other hand, *female* is frequently used for human beings in technical contexts:

> Insurance company actuarial charts indicate that
> females live longer than males

is more precise, if the statistics cover all ages, than

Insurance company actuarial charts indicate that
women live longer than men

And

"The primary reproductive organs or gonads of the
female consist of a pair of ovaries"

is the accepted language of biology and medicine when referring to any vertebrate species, human or otherwise.

This association with medicine, health care, and other insti-
tutional contexts like law enforcement could explain why *female*
and *male* frequently sound a wrong note.

The two female suspects were held on $50,000 bonds

may be the prescribed form for a police report, but in ordinary
writing

Both women were held on $50,000 bonds

is less clinical.

Woman

Obviously, *woman* is the most useful all-around word for referring to an adult female person:

The jury of seven women and five men was chosen
quickly.

Their new advertising campaign is directed at women.

She's an attractive woman with a colorful, confident
style.

For a person somewhere between girlhood and womanhood—
often a variable and subjective state—*woman* can always be qual-
ified by *young,* either when it might sound strange or inappropriate to use *woman* by itself, as in

She's only eleven, but she has the presence of a young
woman,

or when a substitute for *girl* is desirable:

> We are trying to expand our readership to include
> young women in the thirteen- to sixteen-year age-
> group.

One of the problems with *woman* is that, like other female-associated words, it is frequently used as a modifier when no modifier is called for (see page 66ff.). Unlike

> Many women choose to go to a woman doctor, just as
> many men prefer a man doctor,

which makes a valid distinction, *woman* is forever ending up in some mindless cliché like *woman driver,* that implied canard refuted long ago by statistics.

Used as a noun, *woman* connotes independence, competence, and seriousness of purpose as well as sexual maturity. Because these qualities in women are often seen as threatening, some people shy away from the very word, as though it were taboo, and use alternatives like *lady, girl,* and *gal* as euphemisms, especially in conversation and informal writing:

> One of the ladies who was laid off had worked on the
> assembly line for twenty years.

> We met several ladies from St. Louis at our hotel in
> Majorca.

> Did you invite all the gals in the editorial department
> to the party?

Despite this quasi-taboo, however, *woman* has come into its own as a strong, positive term, like *man,* connoting responsible adulthood. A recent study of the qualities people consider typical of a "girl," a "lady," and a "woman" showed that "woman" had by far the most favorable rating, "girl" the least favorable. "The typical lady," the study concluded, "is weaker, less sexy, less intelligent, less of a leader, more dependent, more nervous and more afraid than the typical woman." (See **Reference Notes,** page 172.)

Editor Sey Chassler used *woman* in its cardinal sense when he ended a moving tribute to the late Margaret Mead:

"She was a woman."

WOMEN AND WORK

"Do you talk to a working woman any differently than a housewife?"

—Advertising executive

What are housewives if not working women? Studies have shown that the average housewife works 99.6 hours a week at a wide variety of jobs that are clearly defined in the paid work force—jobs such as purchasing agent, cook, cleaner, economist, and chauffeur—all without pay.

Advertisers, along with other speakers and writers, might achieve better communication with women who are full-time homemakers if they used terms like *salaried women, wage-earning women,* or *women employed outside the home* when referring to women in the paid work force. The executive quoted above might have said

Do you talk to a woman who works outside the home any differently than to a housewife?

It is interesting and probably significant that many women do not use the term *work* to describe their housekeeping or home-making activities. Nor, in general, do members of their families. A woman "stays home" rather than "works at home." She "fixes dinner" rather than "works in the kitchen." In contrast, activities men traditionally undertake around the house are usually dignified by the name *work.* A man "works on the car" or "does his own electrical work." He may have a "workshop" in the basement.

Housewife

While the job a housewife performs is greatly undervalued, the word *housewife* itself is overworked and often used with disparaging connotations. An insurance agency advertises that its agents take the time to explain homeowners' insurance "in terms even a housewife can understand."

The patronizing tone of the ad would be softened if it were revised to read

in terms the average householder can understand.

A newspaper article on the making of an animated motion picture described the vast amount of work required to produce 250,000 separate images on celluloid transparencies:

"On four floors of a Los Angeles office building, more than 150 artists did the actual animating. Two hundred housewives with steady hands did the routine work of painting the images onto cels."

Since steady hands and an aptitude for routine work are less characteristic of housewives as a class than they are of, say, watch repairers, the use of the term *housewives* here is either irrelevant or insulting: this chore is so simple even a housewife can do it. Or perhaps the writer was trying to say that after the salaried artists had completed the animation, another 200 people finished the routine painting at home on a piecework basis. If so, why not say so? If not, a better alternative would have been

Two hundred assistants selected for their steady hands did the routine work. . . .

If, as may well be the case, the real issue involved is low pay and little or no chance for advancement, the heading on the following classified ad says it all:

"HOUSEWIVES WANTED

to work full or part time helping us to make XYZ Lighting Fixtures. Soldering, finishing, packing, wiring. Flexible hours, will train."

Housewife is also usually out of place as a primary descriptive for a woman who does something newsworthy.

The counterfeit credit cards were traced to a 47-year-old Denver housewife gives no more pertinent information than would have been conveyed by "a 47-year-old Denver woman," and it could leave some readers with the impression that a connection exists between housewifery and the use of counterfeit credit cards.

The misuse of *housewife* was epitomized when Margaret Thatcher became prime minister of Great Britain. News and background stories at the time regularly identified her as "a housewife." As it happened, Thatcher, a tax lawyer and former cabinet minister, ran her own household and so was in fact a housewife. To single out that term in describing her, however, was to imply that homemaking was her chief or only skill and the primary reason she was chosen to lead the nation. It is hard to imagine any circumstances in which a comparable reference would be made to a man.

Perhaps the Thatcher example should be taken as evidence of the high esteem in which the Western world holds the homemaker's job. On the contrary. About the same time Thatcher was being described as "a housewife," an American newspaper ran an article about the growing number of men who are now full-time homemakers and headed it "The Nonworkers." If in the eyes of society *housework* and *nonwork* are equated, no wonder so many women whose chosen job is to maintain a home feel obliged to describe their occupation as "just housewife."

Working Wife, Working Mother

"What is a working wife? One whose arms and legs move?"
—An editor

"Working mothers? Are there any other kind?"
—A *Little Leary* cartoon

In a series of articles entitled "Women at Work," a financial newspaper presented much well-researched factual information about women's increased participation in the labor market. But the series also reinforced some common assumptions: first, that it is always preferable in a marriage for the husband to be the breadwinner, the wife to be the homemaker and chief parent;

second, that although it is acceptable for a man to hold a paid job even when he has other, adequate sources of income, a married woman who works outside the home for satisfaction rather than necessity contributes both to the unemployment of others and to growing inequities between rich and poor. Yet by omitting any consideration of the monetary value of homemaking—a figure that can be reckoned according to its replacement cost in the gross national product—the articles strengthened the widespread attitude that the unpaid work homemakers do is not an essential factor in the economy.

Whatever the merits of these assumptions, the language of the series demonstrated how deeply they have become ingrained in our thinking—and therefore in our patterns of writing and speech. This was particularly apparent in the use throughout the series of the terms *working wives* and *working mothers*.

When used to describe someone employed in a paying job, such phrases define a woman primarily in terms of her domestic role; they imply that her main responsibilities are toward something other than her employment. Though the implication is often true, it can be equally true of many men. Yet in the articles men were rarely identified as *working husbands* or *working fathers*.

> "Armed with surveys showing that working wives tend to get more help around the house from husbands . . ."

and, quoting a husband,

> " 'Working wives offer their husbands the flexibility to do what they want with their lives' "

would have been more accurately phrased

> Armed with surveys showing that wives who work outside the home tend to to get more help around the house from husbands . . .

and

> Wives who bring home a paycheck offer their husbands the flexibility to do what they want with their lives.

(In the first instance housework is still assumed to be the wife's responsibility, and in the second she is still assigned a secondary, supporting role; but the language itself is no longer ambiguous.)

An eight-part series on the subject of women in the work force, especially one which drew on many interviews, could probably not be expected to avoid terms like *working wife* or *women who work* completely, and to their credit the writers of the series used many alternatives such as *women holding jobs, women who work for pay, job-holding wife, working parents,* and *the husband-wife working family.* Phrases like *women who work at home* also indicated that work done by full-time homemakers was not being ignored. Nevertheless, the underlying assumption that women belong at home was reinforced by the language of both the writers themselves and the people they quoted.

For example, one woman who works for a tree-spraying company was described by the writer as doing

> "a man's job for equal pay,"

implying that when women compete for better-paid jobs they are invading male territory. However, a later reference in the same article used quotation marks to reflect an awareness—at least on the part of the writer and the women being interviewed —that men do not have exclusive rights to certain jobs:

> "But many working women say they still have to walk softly on the job, particularly if they're doing 'man's work.' "

Women tended to be seen as wives, whereas men were called "men" more often than "husbands." In each of the following sentences *husband* (or *husbands*) would have been the appropriate parallel to *wife* (or *wives*):

> " 'It can be an uncomfortable feeling for a man when his wife goes to work.' "

> "There are some less obvious benefits as well that men might gain through their working wives."

> " 'With a working wife, a man can refuse a transfer, quit his job or just tell his boss to go to hell. . . . A wife's

> job provides a lot of freedom if men are just willing to
> accept it.' "

And so ingrained is the image of woman as wife that she continues to be seen as a wife even when she is divorced:

> "Mrs. Doe, 53, was divorced three years ago. . . . As
> head of a household, [she] is a member of the most
> underprivileged group of working wives."

Married women are seen as blameworthy in a manner not
shared by men—whatever their marital, economic, or job status
—or by unmarried women:

> "Also disturbing are the tensions now arising between
> wives who work because of strict financial need and
> those who work because they want the status,
> satisfaction and adventure of carving a niche in the
> labor market."

Not surprisingly, wives, even when employed full time, are responsible for the smooth running of the household, as in the
example already quoted and in the following:

> "Local repairmen . . . get frequent requests nowadays
> to fix broken appliances after 4 P.M. or on Saturdays,
> because the customers are working wives."

Actually the reason no one is at home is

> . . . because both the husband and wife have jobs,

and

> "the day-time absence of employed wives"

is every bit as much

> the day-time absence of husband and wife, both of
> whom are employed.

Even children tend to be seen as more the mother's children
than the father's. Following a description of youngsters waiting
outside an elementary school before it opens in the morning,
the copy reads

"Occasionally, a teacher or the principal also will come early to mind these offspring of working mothers."

Since the implication was not that these particular children are from single-parent families, but families in which both mother and father are employed, the sentence might have been phrased more equitably:

Occasionally, a teacher or the principal also will come early to mind these children whose parents both have jobs.

When the financial contribution of both spouses is the focus of attention, there is no more reason to single out women as workers (working mothers, working wives) *than to single out men:*

Most of the houses in the new development are being built by two-income families.

A two-paycheck family usually has less trouble getting a mortgage.

Homemaking and Parenting

In the small percentage of one-parent families where the parent is a man, and in two-parent families where both parents are employed, fathers increasingly perform or share the work traditionally done by mothers. In addition, one estimate puts the number of men in the United States who are full-time homemakers at 200,000. Thus the disparity in the once commonly understood meanings of the verbs *to mother* (the social act of nurturance) and *to father* (the biological act of insemination) is disappearing. *Fathering,* too, has acquired the meaning "caring for or looking after someone" previously ascribed only to *mothering,* and a new word, *parenting,* is gaining acceptance.

New words come into being because enough people feel a need for them. *Parenting* serves two purposes: (1) it describes the role of single parents who have to try to be both mother and father to their children, and (2) it de-emphasizes the stereotype so frequently found in two-parent families that only mothers are responsible for "mothering." Like the familiar word *parent-*

hood, parenting conveys a sense of mutuality and shared responsibility.

> Parents can help each other learn the arts of
> mothering and fathering

makes an arbitrary distinction between two prescribed roles. A father's ability to nurture and a mother's experiences in a world wider than the home are not denied when the sentence is rephrased

> Mothers and fathers can help each other learn the art
> of parenting.

The nonsexist goal that I would advocate is not that every profession should consist of half males and half females. . . . It is just very unlikely, it seems to me, that males and females are that symmetric. But that is not at all the point of a push towards sex-neutral language. The purpose of eliminating biases and preconceptions is to open the door wide for people of either sex in any line of work or play. *Symmetric opportunity*, not necessarily symmetric distribution, is the goal that we should seek.

—Douglas R. Hofstadter, *Metamagical Themas*

5

Parallel Treatment

WOMEN AND *MEN*

Nonparallel terminology is common in side-by-side references to the sexes, and it always seems to work one way: at women's expense. When a radio newscaster reported that

"Three Stanford University students—two girls and a man—were abducted from a research station in Africa"

the implication was that the "girls" were less mature than the "man"—or less significant. Yet the sentence could easily have been worded

Three Stanford University students—two women and a man—were abducted from a research station in Africa.

A newspaper reference to members of a hotel housekeeping staff suffers from the same problem:

> "Of course Miss Doe has help; in this case a large staff of men and maids."

Again, the parallel to *men* is *women,* but unless the hotel also employs children, dogs, or robots,

> . . . Miss Doe has . . . a large staff of men and women

provides even less information than the original reference. The traditional parallel to *maids* being *janitors* or *housemen,*

> . . . Miss Doe has . . . a large staff of maids and housemen

would be a step in the right direction. Better, since the sex of the employees is not germane, the writer could have used common-gender job titles (see page 36ff.) and provided additional housekeeping details in the bargain:

> Of course Miss Doe has help; in this case a large staff of room attendants, cleaners, electricians, carpenters, and plumbers.

MAN AND WIFE

Man as a synonym for *husband* was labeled "archaic or colloquial" as long ago as 1913. If a writer were to submit an article containing the sentence

> The governor was accompanied by her man of thirty-eight years and their daughter and son

an editor would undoubtedly change it to read

> The governor was accompanied by her husband of thirty-eight years and their daughter and son.

Yet many writers habitually use the phrase *man and wife* when they mean "husband and wife." In commenting on the outcome of a palimony lawsuit, a newspaper editorial concluded

"The rest of the country should feel challenged at finding that the California courts pay more humane attention to a couple that once lived together outside marriage than courts elsewhere do to man and wife."

No doubt one reason the nonparallel *man and wife* persists is its use in the marriage services of many churches. For example, in the traditional form provided in the Book of Common Prayer the minister says,

"I pronounce that they are Man and Wife"

and a rubric then directs that

"The Man and Wife kneeling, the Minister shall add this Blessing."

What many people are not aware of is that in the beginning of the same service the two people about to be married are referred to as "the Man and the Woman," and it is not until after the actual marriage has taken place that the wording changes to "Man and Wife." Symbolically, two have been made one, but also symbolically the man's status as a person remains intact whereas the woman's is changed from person to role.

In a revision of the Episcopal Church prayer book the celebrant now says,

"I pronounce that they are husband and wife,"

and it is also significant that in this version the well-known injunction

"Those whom God hath joined together let no man put asunder"

now reads

"Those whom God has joined together let no one put asunder."

(However, the traditional order of male before female, maintained throughout the service, has not been altered.)

RELIGIOUS LANGUAGE

> "Dear God,
>
> Are boys better than girls? I know you are one, but
> try to be fair.
>
> Sylvia"

The poignancy of this appeal written by a child captures the deeply felt anguish that many religious women confront throughout their lives: believing themselves to be created in the image of God, they must nevertheless struggle with a sense of personal inferiority because the language of their faith tells them that God is male.

The androcentric bias of English is especially problematic for religious people of both sexes who are deeply devoted to certain traditional forms of worship but who, at the same time, strongly affirm the equality of women and men. Having originated and developed in patriarchal societies, the major Western religions still rely heavily on male imagery to express their understanding of both the Creator and the created. Even when the ancient writings themselves contained female imagery, those who translated the scriptures into English tended to choose male-linked figures of speech in their efforts to evoke the majesty and power of the original texts. These exclusive metaphors were, in turn, incorporated into tradition and worship.

Because many religious organizations have acknowledged the impact of male-centered language on their teachings, a growing number of resources are now available for those attempting to make their prayers, hymns, and other liturgical materials more inclusive. Some of these resources are listed beginning on page 164.

DOUBLE STANDARDS

Describing Women by Appearance

Emphasis on the physical characteristics of women is offensive in contexts where men are described in terms of achievements or character. Although, happily, the time is past when the media reported items like

> The brilliant tax lawyer and his petite blonde secretary
> were arrested Thursday afternoon,

it is still common to come across gratuitous references to a woman's appearance in contexts where similar references to a man would be ludicrous. For example, a reporter, commenting on the favorable impression Mikhail Gorbachev made on a group of legislators who were visiting the Soviet Union, said of Gorbachev,

> "He joked with them; he's relaxed; his wife has pretty ankles."

Had the delegation visited a country where the head of state was a woman, it stretches credulity to imagine the reporter saying,

> She joked with them; she's relaxed; her husband has bulging biceps.

A woman's appearance is still sometimes contrasted with her capabilities as though attractiveness and competence were incompatible:

> "Dolores Doe's calm, quiet demeanor and stunning Filipino beauty belie the fact that she too hopes to finish a Ph.D. during this school year—in nuclear physics."

The disparagement implicit in the writer's astonishment is best demonstrated by imagining the parallel treatment of a man (even when the female-associated physical attribute is changed to a male-associated one):

> Juan Doe's calm, quiet demeanor and stunning Filipino physique belie the fact that he too hopes to finish a Ph.D. . . .

Trivializing

Language used to describe women's actions often implies that women behave more irrationally and emotionally than men.

The writer Gena Corea cites an example of such nonparallel treatment on a network newscast. In a story about a conference on the ordination of women to the Catholic priesthood, a reporter stated that the women began "bickering." Another story on the same newscast concerned a "disagreement" between Israeli and Arab heads of state. In a letter to the network, Corea commented that "it seems women 'bicker' but men 'disagree.' "

Similarly, when a woman asserts herself on a public issue her stand is frequently trivialized by wording that would not be used of a man.

"CITY COUNCILWOMAN
RUFFLED BY ABSENCES"

could easily have been

CITY COUNCILWOMAN
CRITICAL OF ABSENCES

or

ABSENTEEISM IRKS
CITY COUNCIL MEMBER.

Verbs chosen to characterize someone's actions can subtly affect the impression given of the person's effectiveness or forcefulness. Compare, for example,

"Harriet Tubman helped slaves to escape and served as a spy"

with

Harriet Tubman led slaves to freedom and was a spy;

or

She serves as a lobbyist for the tobacco industry

with

She is a lobbyist for the tobacco industry

or

She lobbies for the tobacco industry.

Because women are traditionally perceived to be passive, they fall victim to this particular form of belittlement more often than men.

After being called "the leading lady of lexicography," Alma Graham pointed out that the phrase, though well intended, implied she was playing a role, not doing the job of a bona fide professional. Furthermore, she said, "No one would seek to flatter a man by calling him, say, 'the matinee idol of lexicography.'" As if to underscore her point, William Safire, in need of such a term for a man, once came up with "the rex of lex."

Passive Constructions

The poet June Jordan points out that when women say things like

> "I lost my job" *instead of* "They fired me"

or

> "I was raped" *instead of* "He raped me"

they are contributing to the harmful stereotype of "woman as victim" and, at the same time, absolving someone else of responsibility.

The inference may be different but the suggestion of passivity remains in the expressions

> She had a baby by him

and

> She had his baby,

the origins of which probably go all the way back to the time when men were understood to procreate babies on their own, women being merely the vessels which carried them.

> She had a baby with him

or

> They had a baby

recognizes the dual contribution required.

The effect of a passive construction is sometimes less obvious. When a news story reported

> "The U.S. expedition seeking to put the first American woman atop 29,028-foot Mount Everest was forced to turn back by high winds. . . ."

it was hard not to picture the woman being carried up the mountain like some sort of package, her stalwart male bearers stumbling and falling in their valiant efforts to deposit her on the summit.

Women as Entities, Not Appendages

An entire category of nonparallel linguistic treatment involves the weight given to women's domestic relationships. In a trade journal announcement of the appointments of four men and one woman to executive posts in a large company, each man was described in terms of his previous jobs, without reference to his marital state. The woman's professional background was also given, but only after she had been identified as the widow of a well-known race car driver.

Sometimes the compulsion to identify a woman as someone's wife or widow is doubly gauche, as in this introduction to a capsule book review:

> "Margaret Millar, the widow of Ross Macdonald, has herself been a prolific writer of mystery stories, and recently she won the Grand Master Award from the Mystery Writers of America. Her latest product is. . . ."

The critic then gave Millar's new mystery an unfavorable review. An obvious alternative,

> Margaret Millar, a prolific writer of mystery stories who recently won the Grand Master Award from the Mystery Writers of America, has a new book called. . . .

deals with Millar as writer, not Millar as relict, and—since the review happened to be negative—avoids any insinuation that without Macdonald at her elbow, Millar may not be as good as her public and the Mystery Writers of America once thought.

When the article is about married people who are working as a team, the tendency is to name the male half and then identify the female as his wife, as this caption writer did:

> "Country doctors: Dr. Henry Joe outside his office in
> Rural County, N.J. Dr. Joe's wife, Dr. Janet Coe,
> below, examines a student [at the] elementary school."

Although the reporter who wrote the accompanying story followed convention in putting Dr. Joe's name first, he neatly explained the couple's relationship without making Dr. Coe an appendage:

> "After looking for a country doctor for 20 years, River
> Township got two. Dr. Henry Joe and Dr. Janet Coe,
> who wanted country living, set up shop here in May.
> They were married six years ago."

A married woman can lose her identity entirely when she and her husband are lumped under one name—his. A newsphoto showing two women and two men, all of them huddling under a large plastic sheet as they watch a baseball game in the rain, is captioned:

> "Joe Poe (far right) and Ron Doe (beside him) and
> their wives did not let the rain chase them to cover."

The caption could easily have read:

> Four fans who did not let the rain chase them to cover
> were (left to right) Rose Doe, June Poe, Ron Doe, and
> Joe Poe.

One reason women tend to be identified as somebody's wife is the social custom, which goes back only to the nineteenth century, of calling a married woman by her husband's full name, prefixed by "Mrs." (see **The Social Titles *Mrs., Miss,* and *Ms.,*** page 124). Some women, among them Mrs. Humphry Ward, the writer and antisuffragist, and Mrs. H. H. A. Beach, the composer, even insisted on being known professionally by their husbands' names rather than their own. And although

times are changing, their influence lingers. Rare is the list of sponsors of a money-raising event that doesn't include several women listed as, for example, "Mrs. Joseph P. Blow" and "Mrs. Jerome F. Glow" instead of "Joan M. Blow" and "Mary Gordon Glow."

The custom remains particularly strong today when the woman's husband is better known than she (never mind that she will never be well known if she refuses to establish her own identity), or, if he has died, she feels she is acting in his stead or wishes in this way to memorialize his name. Even when women are better known than their husbands, however, they are often cast in secondary roles by writers who must sense Mesdames Ward and Beach looking over their shoulders. The sentence

> Mrs. Louis Francis, whose husband is a career foreign service officer, is having her third one-woman show at the Connecticut Avenue Gallery. . . .

gets Louis in all right, but does he belong? If a woman's husband's career has a bearing on a story about her, he might be mentioned early on:

> Martha Francis is having her third one-woman show at the Connecticut Avenue Gallery. The painter, whose husband, Louis Francis, is a foreign service officer, has lived in the Far East for many years, and her firm but delicate brush strokes capture . . .

But even under those circumstances, Louis Francis, if he is mentioned at all, probably belongs in the last paragraph rather than the first.

Incidental information about children and grandchildren is also often prominently included in news of women, as though the number of her offspring was the major definer of a woman's life and an indicator of her intellectual or executive competence:

"MOTHER OF 5
TO REPRESENT
STATE STUDENTS

> A Milford mother of five was named to the state Board of Higher Education Monday. . . ."

Was she appointed because anyone with five children is presumed to understand the problems of students? No. As later paragraphs establish, the appointment was made because the woman was herself a part-time student active in several statewide student groups. A more straightforward and informative approach might have been

STUDENT NAMED
TO STATE BOARD
OF EDUCATION

> A Milford woman active in student affairs was named to the state Board of Higher Education. . . .

Another newspaper story, this one reporting on a four-year study of prostitution, identified the sociologist who did the study by her university affiliation, but the next reference to her began

> "Doe, a 35-year-old mother of two who teaches a
> course in deviant behavior . . ."

Was Doe's motherhood mentioned to provide a note of respectability? Or, on the contrary, was there an implied question: what is a *mother* doing studying deviant behavior? Whatever the reason, a similar article about a man would almost certainly omit reference to his fatherhood:

> Roe, 35, who teaches a course in deviant behavior . . .

or would include it only with other biographical material.

Sometimes it seems that when women are identified as wives, mothers, and grandmothers, especially in contexts where men are not identified in similar ways, the message is intended to be that women do things for love, men for profit:

> "Two of the 1,000 inventions patented this week are
> aimed at improving the health and safety of babies.
> One is an alarm belt to monitor an infant's condition
> and reduce crib fatalities. The other, offered by a
> grandmother, is a collapsible outdoor shelter. . . ."

The second paragraph of this newspaper story named the two people (they were men) who had invented the monitor and mentioned their jobs, though not their marital state or relationship to babies. After giving the name and occupation of the inventor of the outdoor shelter, however, the story went on to give her husband's name and occupation and the additional information that she was the mother of three children and the grandmother of two. If these details were included because they were supposed to have a bearing on the invention of a device to protect babies, would not the parenthood and grandparenthood of the two other inventors have been equally apropos?

On some occasions information about a person's children, grandchildren, and spouse is relevant and of genuine interest. In

deciding whether and how to refer to a woman's family relation-
ships, the best test is to ask oneself, "Would I write it this way if
the subject were a man?"

The answer is clear in the case of the following headline and
lead paragraph of a wire service news story, which has been
rewritten to change the sex of the subject, and sex-related
words, but nothing else:

> "COAST GRANDPA, 56,
> DRIVES HEAVY TRUCK
>
> Fulfilling his lifelong dream, John Doe, a 56-year-old
> grandfather of eight, has begun driving a 76,000-
> pound truck and double trailer for a freight company
> full time."

Woman as Metaphor

Words that define women as animals, edibles, or sex objects—
chick, tomato, and *broad* to name some of the milder ones—need
no comment in a book addressed to people interested in nonsexist language. Worth mentioning, however, is a verbal weapon
some men use without, apparently, thinking through its implications.

When a man or boy likens another man or boy to a woman,
he is delivering a double-edged insult: he offends the male,
which is his intention, but he also offends women, a point he
may or may not openly acknowledge. Some years after a lawyer
in New York had called judges "whores" and "madams" in a
magazine interview, he was himself being considered for the
bench. Challenged to explain his remark by one of the judges
reviewing his credentials, the lawyer said, "It was a metaphor,"
and in any case he didn't mean the man who was now asking
for an explanation. Of course. The fact is, however, that the
lawyer had not called judges "pimps" or any other male-identi-
fied word. He had chosen terms almost exclusively applied to
women.

In another case (interesting because again the slur, intended
for publication, was made by a man of professional stature), an
author who had been nominated for a national book award
chose to protest literary prizes in general by saying,

> "It's vulgar and cheap. It's like being asked to put on a
> sequined gown and stepping out to get your Oscar."

Although not one of the eight nominees that year was a woman,
the image of women in sequined gowns accepting awards was
obviously a better metaphor for cheap vulgarity in the author's
mind than men doing the same thing, however costumed.

CATEGORIES

Subconscious attitudes about women are often revealed in the
way a speaker or writer classifies people, as in

> "The crew of the space flight will include two women
> and a Canadian."
> "I trade with doctors, lawyers, all kinds of
> professionals, even females."
> "The honor student, the social worker, and the
> grandmother were all sentenced to eight years in jail."

Or the way they mix women (and other lesser beings) with objects:

> "[Horowitz] will take his wife, Wanda, along with his
> own piano and a piano technician."

Among these "lesser beings" are minority men (you can tell they
are men because their sex isn't specified), as in,

> "The state has elected a black and a woman to high
> office for the first time"

instead of

> In electing a black man and a white woman to high
> office, the state has achieved two firsts: he is the first of
> his race and she the first of her sex to hold important
> statewide posts.

Brevity is lost, but so is the inference that high officeholders are
assumed to be male and white unless otherwise identified.
  Linguists and anthropologists know that people of different
cultures see the world differently at least in part because of the

varied ways their languages classify things and beings. The linguist Mary Ritchie Key, who is particularly interested in groupings in which women occur, observes that "these notional categories . . . are powerful forces behind the actual expressions of language and are based on distinctions which are not regarded as trivial by the speakers of the language." Among the examples she cites are: signs on religious edifices in certain countries announcing that "Women and dogs and other impure animals are not permitted to enter"; the view expressed by a university president, anticipating that a military draft would reduce the number of men in graduate schools, when he said, "We shall be left with the blind, the lame, and the women"; and a magazine's reference to a certain reformer as a "defender of both forms of homosexuality, of Mozart, women's rights, and dumb animals."

I wanted to be an astronaut . . .
but it's "Man's Conquest of Space!"

I wanted to be a doctor . . .
but it's "Man's Fight against Disease!"

I wanted to be the president . . .
but it's "Man's Struggle for Power!"

Now all I want
is a self-cleaning oven.

Librarians are constantly confronted by questions that come up because of the way catalog entries are worded. What, for example, is or is not included in the subject headings *Man, Fossil Man,* or *Manned Space Flight,* or in headings based on the dictum "If it isn't labeled 'female' it's 'male' "? Entries like

Women as Inventors
Women as Seafarers
Women as Theologians

imply in a subtle way that women are not bona fide inventors; that no women have followed the sea for their livelihood; that influential theologians are always male. The addition of *as* is judgmental, raising questions about women's fitness in these areas. Until general knowledge catches up with the way things really are, the form

Women Theologians

may be an unavoidable compromise.

ORDER

The convention of placing males first whenever reference is made to people of both sexes is a deeply embedded habit in writing and speech. It is also a habit that can be broken by conscious effort. A news story by science writer Lawrence K. Altman began

"A West German wife-husband team of doctors has
invented a device that promises to reduce significantly
the number of common birth defects. . . ."

and Altman later named the team as

"Dr. Renate Huch and Dr. Albert Huch of the
University of Marburg."

But despite the refreshing reversal of the usual order, the caption under the accompanying photograph followed the old pattern. Although Renate Huch stands to the viewer's left and her husband to the right, the caption reads

"Dr. Albert Huch and wife, Renate, at Marburg
hospital."

Since English-speaking people are accustomed to reading pic-
tures as we read type, from left to right, why did the caption
writer not opt for

Dr. Renate Huch and Dr. Albert Huch at Marburg
hospital

or, if brevity was essential,

Drs. Renate and Albert Huch at Marburg hospital.

People come up with all sorts of reasons why in word pairs
males almost always come first: *men and women, male and female,
his and hers, boys and girls, guys and dolls,* etc. Some linguists theo-
rize that it is easier to say a single-syllable word like *men* than a
two-syllable word like *women,* and that we tend to put the single
syllable first as a result. Another theory is that the order has
something to do with prosodic patterns: since "men and
women" and "male and female" scan as two trochees, they trip
more lightly off the tongue than they would if reversed to scan
as a trochee and an iamb. Neither theory accounts for *husbands
and wives* or such other familiar phrases as *coffee and cake, needle
and thread, hammer and tongs, fathers and sons,* or—to get to the
root of the matter—*Adam and Eve.*

It seems clear that the convention of male precedence in English followed the same pattern as the arrogation to males of the
Old English word *man* and the grammarians' pronouncement
that *he* is generic. To insure observance of the convention, an
early grammarian, Thomas Wilson, formulated the following
"rule," published in 1553:

Some will set the Carte before the horse, as thus. My mother
and my father are both at home, even as thoughe the good
man of the house ware no breaches, or that the graye Mare
were the better horse. And what thoughe it often so happen-
eth (God wotte the more pitte) yet in speaking at the leaste, let
us kepe a natural order, and set the man before the woman
for maners Sake.

Those who have no stake in maintaining the so-called natural order of the sexes do not set one before the other as a matter of rule; they allow, instead, for variations that come naturally:

> "Search until you find the therapist who believes as much as you do that recovery is possible, and then cherish her or him as you would your most precious possession."

> "Gentlemen and ladies, this is our last class before the spring break."

> "The Point Reyes Light, . . . a 16-page weekly with a circulation of 2,700, is put out by Catherine and David Mitchell, the owners, and one full-time reporter."

NAMES AND TITLES

Women are frequently referred to by their first names in circumstances where men are called by their last names. The impression created, intentionally or not, is that women merit less serious consideration, less respect, or perhaps more paternalistic indulgence than men. An article on the pastels of the artist Alice Barney, which ran in a magazine published by a major museum, referred to her throughout as "Alice," whereas a piece on the work of the painter Henri Rousseau in the same issue consistently called him "Rousseau." A television talk show host, interviewing a female nurse-midwife and a male obstetrician on the question of out-of-hospital births, always addressed the former as "Mary," the latter as "Dr. Green." At the time of the first summit meeting between President Ronald Reagan and Soviet leader Mikhail Gorbachev, a senior associate in Soviet affairs at a prestigious foundation in Washington was quoted as saying of Raisa Gorbachev, "I hear reports from Eastern European diplomats . . . that Raisa has considerable influence on her husband," and another expert, a university professor, told reporters, "People in the Soviet Union do not see Raisa as prominently there as we see Nancy here. . . . [But] we have begun to see her in the background at public events, like showing her seated behind Gorbachev when he gives a speech."

This kind of nonparallel naming is even less appropriate if

the woman referred to is herself a national leader. When Corazon Aquino came to power in the Philippines, many in the
media automatically adopted her nickname, as in:

"There is no certainty that Cory's army will be more
effective than Marcos'."

Since referring to Ferdinand Marcos as "Ferdinand" (much less
"Ferdy") would hardly be an acceptable alternative, the sentence
—and a hundred similar ones—could as easily have used the
last names of both:

There is no certainty that Aquino's army will be more
effective than Marcos'.

The tendency today is for politicians and other public figures
to encourage the use of their first names: "Call me Ella"; "Run,
Jesse, Run"; "Elect Sam"; "Cor-ee! Cor-ee!" But it is not at all
likely that in serious news coverage the press would take the
liberty of first-naming an important man.

When two people being discussed have the same surname,
solving the problem of parallel treatment may be a little more
difficult, though a solution is not usually hard to find. In a
profile of a Washington-based columnist we will call James J.
Morgan, the author has this to say of Sylvia Morgan, James
Morgan's wife:

"Sylvia seldom spoke during the smaller dinner parties
that became Morgan's greenest playing field, but
Morgan sparkled."

If the pair referred to had been brothers with the same last
name, the sentence would probably have read:

John Morgan seldom spoke during the smaller dinner
parties that became his brother's greenest playing field,
but James Morgan sparkled

or

John seldom spoke . . . but James sparkled,

and either solution would have worked equally well in writing
about James and Sylvia Morgan's dinner-party demeanor.

A BUSINESS TALE

Bill's attempts to interest XYZ Company in his products had finally paid off.

He was invited to make a presentation and was offered the use of a conference room in a letter signed John Liveridge, assistant to the president.

When Bill signaled that he was set up, a woman and a man entered the room.

The woman said to Bill, "I'm Virginia Hancock, and this is John Liveridge, my . . . "

Bill enthusiastically broke in, drowning her last word, "I'm delighted to meet you, Mr. Liveridge, and you too, Ginny."

Ms. Hancock owned the company, Mr. Liveridge was her assistant, and Bill lost a customer.

—Pearl G. Aldrich, *Nation's Business*

The deeply ingrained custom of identifying women by social titles sometimes results in subtle distinctions. When the Supreme Court handed down its decision that pension plans which pay women less than men are illegal, a wire service dispatch reported:

> "[Justice Thurgood] Marshall's opinion . . . was joined
> by Justices Brennan, White, Stevens and Mrs.
> O'Connor. Dissenting were Chief Justice Warren E.
> Burger and Justices Powell, Blackmun and Rehnquist."

Good grief! Who is that ringer who had the gall to add her two-cents-worth to the weighty opinions of all those justices? Since Supreme Court Justice Sandra Day O'Connor's social title is out of place in this context, using it is both irrelevant and confusing. The obvious wording also happens to be the simplest:

> Marshall's opinion . . . was joined by Justices Brennan,
> White, Stevens, and O'Connor.

Unfortunately, the use of "Mrs. O'Connor" in the example above was not a simple lapse of good editorial judgment. The wire service originating the report has a policy requiring that titles be dropped after the initial reference—men's titles, that is. Women's professional titles are also dropped, but in their case social titles are substituted. Thus Justice Sandra Day O'Connor becomes Mrs. O'Connor, Lieut. Helen Wong becomes Miss (or Ms. or Mrs.) Wong, and Dr. Dora Flora becomes Ms. (or Miss or Mrs.) Flora. "Let's see, now," the reader ends up asking. "Is Ms. Flora the same person who was just named dean of the medical school, or did I miss a beat somewhere? Surely she must be an M.D., but maybe. . . . "

Many people regret the growing editorial practice of dropping titles, whether social or professional, once the person referred to has been identified, but that is another issue. The point here is that whatever policy is adopted, it should be applied across the board.

The same consistency is needed when both members of a husband-and-wife team have academic or professional titles. A magazine article about a pharmacologist included the information that his wife is a physiologist. Both have Ph.D.s and hold academic appointments. But a picture accompanying the article was captioned:

> "Dr. and Mrs. Doe at home with their two-year-old
> Irish setter, Jennie."

If the article had been primarily about the physiologist, would a picture of her with her husband have been captioned "Dr. and Mr. Doe . . . " or "Mr. and Dr. Doe . . . "? One assumes not.

> The Drs. Doe at home with their two-year-old Irish
> setter, Jennie

would have been fine.

Nor, when a wife and husband who have chosen to use the same last name work together professionally, does it mean that she forswears an identity of her own. Although

> Mr. and Mrs. Arthur Gelb

may be an accepted way to address a formal wedding invitation, the authors of *O'Neill*, the definitive biography of the playwright Eugene O'Neill, are

> Arthur and Barbara Gelb.

If a writer does not bother to give the first name of a woman who has taken her husband's surname on marriage, her identity can be obscured or even lost.

> "[A] single citizen can still count—like Mrs. Klussman,
> who saved the San Francisco cable car in the 40s, and
> Dr. A. J. Haagen-Smit, the first man to prove that
> smog is not a byproduct of nature but is chemically
> created in the atmosphere. . . . "

Who was "Mrs. Klussman," and how can one find out more about her? It could have taken only a little effort for the writer to discover her full name and so give parallel credit to two noteworthy activists:

> . . . like Friedel Klussman, who saved the San Francisco
> cable car . . .

Women in the arts and professions have for years used their own names (that is, a family name, a previously held surname, or an adopted name) rather than a husband's surname. Today more women than ever before are making the same choice. Yet journalists often seem reluctant to respect their wishes, with such awkward results as

> "These are sentiments that Martin Ritt, the director,
> and Irving Ravetch and Harriet Frank Jr. (Mrs.
> Ravetch), his screenwriters, understand and fervently
> evoke. . . ."

and later in the same review

> "Mr. Ritt and the Ravetches, who've been collaborating
> on films since. . . ."

In addition to being a collaborator with her husband on screen-plays, Harriet Frank Jr. is an established writer and novelist. Professionally she is neither "Mrs. Ravetch" nor one of "the Ravetches." If the film critic quoted thought it was essential to mention the Frank-Ravetch conjugal relationship, the earlier sentence might have begun

> These are the sentiments that Martin Ritt, the director,
> and the husband-and-wife screenwriting team of
> Irving Ravetch and Harriet Frank Jr. understand and
> fervently evoke. . . .

and the second might have read

> Mr. Ritt, Mr. Ravetch, and Ms. Frank have been
> collaborating on films since. . . .

How serious the consequences of an arbitrary name change can be is illustrated by the case of a woman in politics who married during an election campaign. Because some news-papers then insisted on referring to her by her husband's name rather than the one familiar to her constituents, she was forced to go to court to protect her right to be called by the name of her choice.

A familiar journalistic practice in reports of accidents, arrests, and other unhappy events is exemplified by

> Smith was hospitalized with leg fractures, and the
> Jones woman was treated for minor injuries and
> released.

The usage may stem from an old-fashioned reluctance to call a woman by her last name alone, but the effect is demeaning. Reference is sometimes made also to "the Jones girl," "the Jones boy," even "the Jones dog," but one would rarely, if ever, read that

> Smith was hospitalized with leg fractures, and the Jones man was treated for minor injuries and released.

THE SOCIAL TITLES *MRS., MISS,* AND *MS.*

Mrs., Miss, and *Ms.* are all abbreviations for the now-outdated social title *Mistress.* In the seventeenth and eighteenth centuries the oldest of the three, *Mrs.,* was commonly used before the family name (or given and family name) of an adult woman, whether she was single or married. The same was true of the less common abbreviation *Ms.* (See **Reference Notes,** page 172.) *Miss* as a social title was limited to female children, although as a noun it had the second meaning—as did *mistress*—of "concubine" or "prostitute."

Sometime in the late eighteenth century the social title *Miss* began to be used to distinguish single women from married women, and in the nineteenth century the custom developed of prefixing *Mrs.* to a man's first and last names to identify his wife. In this way, over a period of years, a system evolved by which women, unlike men, were designated "single," "married," "divorced." In the heyday of naming etiquette, for example, Miss Beatrice Hansen became Mrs. Joseph O'Malley when she and Joseph O'Malley were married, and she became Mrs. Hansen O'Malley (or, less formally, Mrs. Beatrice O'Malley) if they were divorced.

The dissatisfaction of many women with this labeling system led eventually to the widespread use of *Ms.,* which appeared in secretarial handbooks in the 1940s as a title analogous to *Mr.* The American Heritage Dictionary defines *Ms.* as "A title of courtesy used before a woman's surname or before her given name and surname, without regard to her marital status," and it gives the plural as *Mses.* or *Mss.* Most current dictionaries contain similar definitions, and the usage is almost universally accepted by the media.

Misunderstanding of the purpose of *Ms.* has occasionally resulted in uses like

Ms. Walter Klein is chairwoman of the committee.

If circumstances called for an honorific, the form would be

Ms. Dorothy Klein.

Although the *Mrs./Miss* distinction is not a reliable indicator of whether or not a woman is married (she may continue to use *Miss* after marriage or, if divorced, may continue to use the title *Mrs.*), many people, including many women, feel strongly that these older titles should be retained, as the following verse attests:

> *In typing* Ms. *for* Mrs.
> *Your Smith Corona slipped.*
> *I am a wife and mother*
> *And not a manuscript.*

Others do not care. Still others are strongly committed to *Ms.* or would prefer no title at all. As another versifier put it:

> *When you call me* Miss *or* Mrs.
> *You invade my private life,*
> *For it's not the public's business*
> *If I am, or was, a wife.*

Because many people do feel strongly about social titles, the obvious and courteous solution for anyone writing* about *a particular woman is to follow her preference. (See **Salutations in Letters,** on the next page, for a discussion of writing *to* women). If the writer does not know or cannot guess what that preference is, the simplest way out is to use no title in the first reference and her last name without title thereafter:

Dorothy Klein is chairwoman of the committee.
Yesterday Klein said . . .

A growing trend is to drop social titles entirely for both women and men. In fact the absence of a social title, as in this example from an author's preface, sometimes becomes a mark of distinction:

> "I wish to thank my colleagues Jane Doe and John Roe who read the manuscript and gave me many valuable suggestions, and Mrs. Mary Poe whose patience in deciphering my handwriting and typing the many drafts required to finish this work was infinite."

SALUTATIONS IN LETTERS

Year after year the popular and authoritative *World Almanac* carried the following note under the heading "Forms of Address":

> "The salutation Dear Sir is always permissible when addressing a person not known to the writer."

In the 1979 edition the note changed:

> "The salutation Dear Sir or Dear Madam is always permissible when addressing a person not known to the writer."

A victory for common sense. Addressing a letter "Dear Sir or Dear Madam" is cumbersome, however, and retains the traditional order.

> Dear Madam or Sir

has the advantage of brevity. The order is alphabetical, but anyone who likes to play the odds is free, of course, to indulge their hunches either way. (Also see *Madam,* page 141.)

"Gentlemen," the usual plural of the traditional "Dear Sir" salutation, lends itself comfortably to the more inclusive

> Gentlemen and Ladies.

As in the previous example, the alphabetical order can be reversed without strain. Also favored by some is the sex-neutral variation

Gentlepeople.

A more conventional solution in addressing an unknown person or group of people is to use the title of the job or group:

Dear Credit Manager
Dear Director of Admissions
Dear Members of the Gaming Commission (*or* Dear Commissioners).

This salutation also works when writing to a company:

Dear Grumble Brothers
Dear North Pole Airlines.

A form letter addressed to individuals in a category often suggests its own salutation:

Dear Homeowner
Dear Friend of the Library.

A school that sends an occasional newsletter to students' homes using the salutation

Dear Mother

might improve communication with many of its readers by using

Dear Parent or Guardian.

Anyone who feels that "dear" is unduly affectionate has the alternative either of omitting any salutation, instead going from the inside address directly to the body of the letter, or of framing the letter as a memo:

To the Credit Manager, Grumble Brothers
To the President, North Pole Airlines.

When the person addressed is known to the writer the degree of formality in the salutation depends, of course, on their relationship. If the addressee is a woman and the writer is uncertain which, if any, social title she prefers (see **The Social Titles *Mrs.*, *Miss*, and *Ms.*,** on page 124), addressing her by her first and last names is always acceptable:

Dear Catherine Castille.

A professional or academic title, if she has one, takes precedence over a social title:

Dear Dr. Castille
Dear Professor Castille
Dear Senator Castille.

For women to become visible, it is necessary that they become linguistically visible. . . . New symbols will need to be created and old symbols will need to be recycled and invested with new images if the male hold of language is to be broken. As the language structure which has been devised and legitimated by male grammarians exacts ambiguity, uncertainty, and anomie for females, then in the interests of dismantling the muted nature of females, that language structure and those rules need to be defied.

—Dale Spender, *Man Made Language*

[W]hen women change the language structure and their language use, they are in fact taking action to change their status in society. They are challenging the legitimacy of the dominant group. By calling the challengers and their proposals for language change silly, unnatural, irrational, and simplistic, the dominant group tries to reaffirm its social identity in the face of a threat.

—Cheris Kramarae, *Women and Men Speaking*

6

A Few More Words

ALUMNAE, ALUMNI

The plural of the feminine-gender word *alumna* is *alumnae;* the plural of the masculine-gender word *alumnus* is *alumni.* These atypical English words, taken over from classical Latin without any change in spelling, have no common-gender forms.

Predictably, men who graduate from an institution that formerly enrolled only women object to being called "alumnae," whereas women who graduate from any institution attended by men are expected to acquiesce in being called "alumni." When a seventy-year-old school of nursing graduated its first male student a few years ago, the Alumnae Association immediately changed its name to Alumni Association.

Vassar was more respectful of its own long tradition as a women's college when in 1969 its Alumnae Association voted to become the Alumnae and Alumni of Vassar College. The following year, however, the association's bylaws were amended to change all nonspecific uses of *alumnae* to *alumni*, "it being understood that the word 'alumni' is both masculine and feminine." That reasoning may not have cut much ice with alumnae who learned their Latin at Vassar, for the bylaws as further amended in June 1985 use the telescoped term *alumnae/i* for all nonspecific references.

Many other women who went to schools and colleges that later became coeducational do not accept the assumption that *alumni* is both masculine and feminine. Nor did the people who spoke Latin as their native tongue. On the contrary, Roman lawmakers deliberately included both the masculine- and feminine-gender forms of all personal nouns and pronouns in wording laws that applied to both men and women. (See **Reference Notes,** page 172.)

Women who object to being called "alumni" may be challenged on the grounds that words frequently change their meanings, and this one can presumably expand to become an umbrella term for both sexes. Perhaps it can, if it is forced, but it would be one more case of subsuming women under "generic" terms that are really masculine-gender words. When men demur at being called "alumnae," their sensibilities are respected, and women deserve the same courtesy, as many educational institutions now recognize. A firm that publishes directories of graduates and former students for many colleges throughout the United States reports that most coeducational institutions are using

Directory of Alumni and Alumnae *(or the reverse order)*.

The abbreviation

alumnae/i *(or the other way around)*

is widely used in print, and some people have even cut the Gordian knot by opting for the bobtailed

alums.

BLOND/BLONDE AND SIMILAR IMPORTS

When English took over the masculine-gender French words *blond* and *brunet,* it also annexed their feminine-gender counterparts *blonde* and *brunette* and acquired in the process special, nonstandard English nouns to use of females: "He is a blond. She is a blonde."

Unlike *alumnus* and *alumna,* where sex-differentiated endings from Latin mark both terms, the seemingly innocuous difference between *blond* and *blonde* becomes in English the difference between the standard (male) and the deviation (female). Why not *blond* for both women and men?

Similar words from the French that still have nonstandard (for English) feminine-gender endings are *fiancé/fiancée* and *divorcé/divorcée.* Although English dictionaries define both forms of *fiancé,* it is significant that many define only the feminine-gender form *divorcée,* indicating our society's predilection for labeling a woman's marital circumstances more frequently than a man's.

We are creatures of habit, of course, but in the interest of simplicity and logic the common-gender forms *blond, brunet, fiancé,* and *divorcé* would seem to suffice for everybody.

COED

This word entered American English around the turn of the century as derisive slang. It exemplified the scorn and hostility directed at women who chose to invade male bastions of higher learning. Even after the idea of higher education for women became widely accepted, *coed* as a noun retained a connotation of frivolity that continues to impair the image of women as serious students.

The word is rarely used as a noun in a strictly academic context. To speak of a Rhodes scholar as a "coed," for example, would belittle both the individual and the award. Associating the term with physical descriptions, as in

> the slim dark coed

or

> a bevy of beautiful coeds

contributes to its trivializing effect. *Coed* is particularly out of place when used of women who are victims of crime or violence:

> "The defendant is being tried for the murder of two coeds."

> "The twenty-year-old coed was kidnapped and buried alive."

> "The University . . . is offering . . . sessions on coping with grief for students mourning the deaths of five sorority coeds killed in a traffic accident."

The use of *coed* is often justified on the grounds that it gives more information than either *woman* alone (which omits the person's status as a student) or *student* (which omits the person's sex). True. But in the examples above the speaker could easily have used both. If males had been the subjects, would anyone cavil at having to use extra words to explain either that they were also students or that the students referred to were male?

As an abbreviation for *coeducational,* the adjective *coed* is a useful one to describe an institution or program for students of both sexes:

> Clarke College, founded as a women's college in 1843, is now coed.

But unless it is also used evenhandedly of males and females, *coed* as a noun will continue to be still another term that defines women as aberrations.

ESQ.

The courtesy title *esquire,* which in some parts of the United States is used in abbreviated form after the name of a practicing attorney, is as appropriate for a woman as for a man—although this view is still not universally accepted.

One side of the question was set forth in the pages of the *Denver Post* when a group of lawyers in that city argued that inasmuch as *esquire* "originally referred to a knight's attendants or members of the English landed gentry, its gender is clearly male and [it] should apply only to men." One of the attorneys went on to propose that the "proper" form for a woman to use was *esquiress*.

In musing on such reasoning, the linguist Alette Hill points out "that it doesn't seem to matter to them that male attorneys on this side of the Atlantic are neither 'knight's attendants' nor 'members of the English gentry.' Their argument for preserving the title for themselves seizes on one component of the medieval title—sex—and ignores the others—national origin and membership in a particular socio-economic class." She makes the point that "This kind of logic is both linguistically naïve and unconvincing. 'Esquire' can be extended to women lawyers in the U.S. since the male attorneys who have been pleased to use it are themselves many centuries and thousands of miles away from its 'true' or 'original' meaning."

As for *esquiress*, such a word was indeed used in the sixteenth and seventeenth centuries, according to the Oxford English Dictionary. It was applied in one case to a mourner, in another to a woman who washed clothes, and in still another to "a small slave girl." "Are we to appeal to these precedents," Hill asks, "as the 'true' or 'correct' term for American women who are members of the bar?"

The contemporary use of esquire *clearly illustrates the linguistic reality that what a word once meant does not necessarily determine what it means today, and, further, that what it means today may not resemble earlier meanings even remotely.*

FELLOW

Fellow, like *guy,* is a word whose appropriateness when used of a woman is being debated: is it so loaded with male associations that it has lost its usefulness as a common-gender noun, or is it one of those terms, like *actor* (see pages 136–137), that women are reclaiming?

Fellow went through a long period when it was used primarily of males, perhaps because the compound *fellowman* suffered the same narrowing of meaning as *man* itself. But during its early history (*fellow* dates from Old English) the word was not so restricted. It meant, according to the Oxford English Dictionary, "a partner, colleague, co-worker." It was also used in the sense of "companion" or "spouse." In Shakespeare's *The Tempest*, Miranda says,

> "I am your wife, if you will marry me . . . to be your fellow. . . ."

True, no one today says, "I'm going out with the fellows tonight," when referring to women, although a woman might conceivably say, "I'm going out with my fellows," meaning her teammates or coworkers. And most people feel comfortable saying, "She's a good fellow."

Since *fellowship, fellow worker,* and *fellow member,* have never been limited to one sex, and most women who receive academic fellowships are called "fellows," one can make a reasonable case that all forms of the word—with the exception of *fellowman*—can be used sex-inclusively.

The problem with *fellowman* comes not from *fellow* but from the protean term *man,* which is sometimes intended to include everyone, sometimes to include males only (see Chapter 1). This ambiguity often surfaces in election years when those running for office become more careful than usual about their language. Then, for example,

> I would like to be of service to my fellowman

is apt to be corrected in mid-sentence to

> —that is, to my fellow citizens.

"FEMININE" SUFFIXES

> Being called a "poetess" brings out the terroristress in me.
> —Adrienne Rich

Most English agent-nouns—words like *teacher, farmer, patron, poet,* etc., which describe someone who does something—have common gender and so can be used of a person of either sex. When French or Latin feminine-gender suffixes like -*ess* and -*trix* are attached to these words to designate women, even if the addition is intended as a courtesy, the basic form acquires a predominantly masculine sense with the unavoidable implication that the feminine-gender form represents a nonstandard variation. Once again the male is identified as the norm, the female as an aberration.

Readers would be shocked to come upon the sentence

The museum is showing the works of a sculptor and a black sculptor.

Yet statements like the following are widely accepted:

The museum is showing the works of a sculptor and a sculptress.

Just as in Western societies the absence of color identification for one of two sculptors in the first example implies that whiteness is the standard, so the absence of sex identification for one of two sculptors in the second implies that maleness is the standard. The sentence can simply read

The museum is showing the works of two sculptors.

A century ago some people considered words like *sculptress, manageress,* and *proprietress* to be complimentary because they emphasized the achievement of a woman pursuing an activity unusual for a person of her sex. As arbitrary limitations on the activities of both women and men have given way, however, so has the fad of female-distinguishing labels. Yet some old-fashioned suffixed words remain popular. When it comes to stereotyping "wicked" females, for instance, -*ess* endings—as in *adultress, temptress, villainess, murderess, bitch-goddess,* etc.—have affixed themselves like leeches. Apparently these terms, to borrow the fanciful words of one magazine essayist, "foster the illusion of woman as Eve, forever volatile and treacherous." In recent years "feminine" suffixes have also reappeared in more neutral labels, and in contexts so strained as to suggest they are being used, consciously or unconsciously, to undermine the prestige of the woman named: a magazine identified Gloria Steinem as an "editress"; a newspaper referred to Leonore Annenberg as "the U.S. Chieftess of Protocol"; an article about Dwight Eisenhower described Kay Summersby as his "wartime chauffeurette"; and many writers and commentators call women like Elizabeth Cady Stanton and Susan B. Anthony "suffragettes" (see pages 150–151).

It is especially revealing that women ordained to the Episcopal priesthood are sometimes referred to as "priestesses" by those who oppose women's ordination. The Episcopal Church in the United States does not have "priestesses"; it has "priests," an order now open to people of both sexes.

For different reasons, *Goddess* and *Creatrix* have recently seen increased usage among people who want to call attention to the once widespread worship of a supreme deity conceived of as female. For others, however, the use of such terms implies that *God* and *Creator* refer to a male deity, a concept most thoughtful religious people reject as idolatrous.

A closer look at each of the feminine-gender suffixes imported into modern English makes their sexist implications clear:

-Ess

The terms *princess, duchess,* and *countess* are little changed from the French versions of those words that entered English as a result of the Norman Conquest in the eleventh century, and they will probably be with us as long as titles of nobility are applicable. Common English words with *-ess* endings, like *actress, waitress, patroness,* and *stewardess,* however, are more recent inventions and carry the implication of "nonstandard," as can be seen from the history of the term *actress.*

When women first began to act on the English stage in the seventeenth century, *actor* (in the sense of a theatrical player) had been in use for about seventy-five years, and women, too, were initially called "actors." A few decades later, *actress* was coined to distinguish females in the acting profession from males, but no comparable new term was introduced to designate the latter. Thus *actor* regained a specific masculine sense and at the same time—as in "actors' guild"—continued to be used as the generic term covering both sexes. Today it is noteworthy that many women in the theater and films are beginning to take back the term *actor*, using it in reference to themselves and other women.

> "Irene Worth . . . one of the world's finest classical actors."

> "Cleo Kocol . . . a writer, an actor, and a humanist activist."

> " 'Some plays I hated and some I loved," Miss Stapleton said, laughing. 'It was refreshing for an actor's needs.' "

Some *-ess* endings present problems for equal opportunity employers. For example, a newspaper help-wanted column headed "Male and Female" includes an ad beginning

> "Waitresses needed both full and parttime . . ."

Since men are unlikely to apply for a job termed *waitress* (and women are not apt to apply at this time for a job with the male-associated label *waiter*) many restaurants are using titles like *server* or *table server*. Another possibility is to adopt a new but recognizable term, as one Boston restaurant has done: a note on its menu says, "Ask your waitron about today's special." In time, *waiter* will probably become an accepted common-gender noun, like *writer*.

Hostess, used in the sense of someone who greets people in a restaurant and leads them to a table, poses a similar difficulty. Women who host radio and television shows are called "hosts," not "hostesses," a precedent that suggests the same term might be used for restaurant employees of both sexes who greet patrons—of both sexes, of course. (The "nonstandard" sense conveyed by the *-ess* suffix is nicely demonstrated by one popular current dictionary that gives as its first definition of *host* "One who entertains guests . . . ," and then defines *hostess* as "A woman who acts as a host.")

Most airlines have dropped the *stewardess/steward* distinction in favor of the common-gender *flight attendant.*

Attached to proper nouns, *-ess* endings are especially offensive. Fortunately *Negress, Jewess, Quakeress,* etc., are almost defunct today (and it is interesting to note in passing that no one ever came up with *whitess, WASPess,* or *Protestantess*).

-Ette

This suffix occurs in French words of feminine gender that have nothing to do with sex, such as *estafette* ("messenger"), *motocyclette* ("motorcycle"), and *gâchette* ("trigger"). Transposed to English, however, the suffix signifies only three things: small size, as in *kitchenette;* imitation, as in *leatherette;* or, when applied to a person, a female imitation of the "real thing," as in *farmerette* and *majorette.*

-Trix

The Latin feminine-gender suffix *-trix* is sometimes tacked onto common-gender English nouns, despite—or perhaps because of—its pretentious sound. The archaic *executrix* and *administratrix* are still used in legal documents, but discerning writers and speakers now avoid such affectations as *narratrix* and *aviatrix,* and there is no reason why *executrix* and *administratrix* cannot also be dropped—anguished cries from lawyers notwithstanding.

Of all the techniques for avoiding linguistic sexism, none is simpler than using the same agent-nouns for both sexes. Neither sex has a monopoly on jobs or the designations that go with them—except in the case of wet nurse, sperm donor, and what has come to be known as "surrogate mother."

FEMINIST

Yes, I call myself a feminist in that I believe there are cultural, social and economic boundaries set for women which are immoral and unnecessary and which should be resisted publicly and privately.

—Elizabeth Hardwick

In Elizabeth Hardwick's definition, *feminist* has a clear, positive meaning, one that most current dictionaries reflect. Yet some writers and speakers invest the word with other connotations, many of them neither positive nor clear. An art critic, describing an exhibit of works by women, managed to impute a sense of "un-American" to *feminist:*

> "Though it has feminist passages, this cannot be said to
> be a feminist show. In fact, it is titled 'American Art:
> American Women,' and the catalogue cover features
> bars of red, white and blue."

In his next sentence, however, the writer confirms the very circumstances that support the usefulness of *feminist* in its widely accepted sense:

> "The fact that so many artists of stature agreed to
> participate in an all-woman show—which often means
> an underdog show—emphasizes that women's
> achievements have again to be underscored."

A recent study of how college students of both sexes interpret *feminist* (see **Reference Notes,** page 173) confirms the positive connotations recorded by lexicographers. By and large, the students saw "a feminist" as "more aggressive, extroverted, more of an activist . . . forceful, ambitious, independent," etc., than the opposites of those criteria, as well as "more logical, knowledgeable, realistic, intelligent, caring, flexible, comforting, good, and fascinating." All in all, not a bad profile.

HERO, HEROINE

The word *hero* applies to males and females alike; the word *heroine,* although it has a long, honorable history going back to the Greek *heroine* (counterpart of the masculine-gender *heros*), is anomalous. Its use today presents the same problem as any other English word used specifically of a female when no comparable masculine-gender term exists: it makes females nonstandard. Although it is possible to say

America's heros include Mother Theresa, Bruce Springsteen, and Madonna,

it is not possible to say

America's heroines include Mother Theresa, Bruce Springsteen, and Madonna.

When President Ronald Reagan honored four young people in his State of the Union address, including a twelve-year-old girl who had risked her life to save the life of another, he referred to them all as "heroes." Similarly, the headline

"SALLY RIDE: HERO FOR OUR TIME"

makes a strong, unequivocal statement, whereas the heading

"HEROINES OF ASTRONOMY"

in an article discussing Caroline Herschel, Maria Mitchell, Annie Jump Cannon, and several other astronomers who were women does not clearly establish whether the writer thinks of them as important in their own right or as notable mainly because they were women who worked in a field dominated by men. This ambiguity is heightened because the suffix -*ine*, which means "pertaining to," suggests a relationship to something rather than independent existence. It occurs in adjectives like *alpine, canine,* and *masculine,* and in a number of patriarchal names like *Pauline, Ernestine,* and *Josephine.*

A reference to Belgian patriot Gabrielle Petit (1893–1916) as a

"spy and national heroine"

leaves as much to be desired semantically as a law passed not long ago in Massachusetts making Deborah Sampson, who fought as a soldier in the Revolutionary War,

"Official Heroine of the Commonwealth."

Once again, use of the sex-limited *heroine* suggests that Deborah Sampson and Gabrielle Petit may not have been especially heroic when judged according to some universal standard by which men would be judged, but rather that they were unusually heroic *for women.*

The difference between using *hero* for both sexes and *man* for both sexes is a practical one.

> Joan of Arc was a hero

is a clear and comprehensive assertion; modern English renders meaningless a statement like

> Joan of Arc was a brave man.

On the Fastrack

MADAM

The salutation *madam* and its less formal variant *ma'am* are in danger of being lost through the process of semantic degradation: because *madam* is also understood to mean "the female head of a house of prostitution," people are afraid to use it in other ways. (Indeed, *madam* can always be manipulated to produce a titter, as a television personality demonstrated in a feature segment on Melina Mercouri when he said she played the part of a prostitute in the film *Never on Sunday* "and now she's a madam—Madam Minister of Culture.")

Judith Martin, a.k.a. Miss Manners, will have none of this. As she wrote in her column:

> As of right now, Miss Manners will permit no further giggling at the word "Madam." . . . Whenever "Mr." is used, for direct

spoken address in combination with certain job titles (Mr. President, Mr. Vice President, Mr. Secretary), the female equivalent is "Madam."

It is a solid-sounding word, unaffected by the office holder's marital status, and—in keeping with the American tradition of simplicity—as appropriate to a private citizen as to a woman of rank. Well-brought-up Southern children still call adult women "Ma'am," which is equally correct for addressing the queen of England to her face. And "Madam" (or "Ma'am")—not "Honey," "Baby," "Tootsie," "Miss" or "Hey, lady!"—is the proper term for a woman whose name one does not know.

Then why are the boys in the back snickering? . . . "Madam," gentlemen, is no longer funny.

We are not going to lose this very proper term because of anybody's improper thoughts, the way we lost the once useful and respectable title "Mistress."

So remember Miss Manners next time you want to attract the attention of the woman who has inadvertently locked her car without turning off the lights. All you need to do is sing out across the parking lot, "Ma'am! You left your lights on!" And when you want to address the woman who is conducting a formal meeting, you can get to your feet and say: "Madam chair, I move that we approve the minutes as read"—or whatever it is you have on your mind. (See also **Salutations in Letters,** page 126.)

MAIDEN

This poetic term evokes the image of a young woman, usually beautiful, possibly dressed in Elizabethan costume, perhaps curtsying or blushing or fainting, and nearly always in need of a male protector. As a noun, *maiden* has had several other meanings, including an eighteenth-century washing machine and a guillotinelike instrument used in Scotland for beheading people in the sixteenth and seventeenth centuries.

In its most common use today, as an adjective, the word expresses, and none too subtly, the cultural view that marriage is a woman's prime destiny. *Maiden* is defined as "unmarried" (said only of women), "virgin," "fresh," "unused," and "intact," as well as "inexperienced" and "untried." To call a woman a "maiden lady" or a "maiden aunt" may seem less pejorative than calling her an "old maid," but it reflects much the same assumption that leads to calling a racehorse of either sex which has never won a race a "maiden horse." The Oxford English Dictionary's long entry on the figurative uses of *maiden* begins with the definition "That has yielded no results." In this sense the word designates a court session at which no cases are tried and a period in a cricket game in which no runs are scored, along with metal that has never been worked and soil that has never been ploughed.

Although the analogies are less judgmental when *maiden* is used to mean "first" or "earliest," as in a ship's "maiden voyage" or a new legislator's "maiden speech" in the legislature, the other connotations of the word are enough to vitiate its meaning when applied to present-day women. Even the patriarchal idea that a woman has a "maiden name" is losing standing: many people now prefer the alternative expression "birth name," which also appears in the civil codes of several states that have statutes concerning the use or restoration of a woman's "birth name or former name."

MASTER

Clifton Fadiman, reviewing a novel by Helen MacInness, wrote:

> "In her field she is a master. In fact she may well be *the* master."

Once the masculine-gender counterpart of *mistress, master* is no longer limited to males except in the rare instances where it is still used as a courtesy title for young boys.

As a verb ("She mastered calculus and trigonometry") and an adjective ("She is a master landscape architect"), the word has long since outgrown its masculine-gender origins. Nevertheless, some writers, unlike Clifton Fadiman in the example above, hesitate to use it as a noun when referring to a woman. A reviewer who wrote of a book by Doris Lessing,

> "This superb anthology of short stories by a current
> master (mistress?) of the genre . . ."

not only distracted the reader's attention foolishly but depre-
cated Lessing's abilities. Although *mistress* retains a sense of authority in some of its definitions (as in "headmistress of a
school"), it has acquired no associations with exceptional skill or
achievement. It occurs most often today in contexts like

> "The former mistress of the defendant will continue
> her testimony. . . ."

Having few uses not better served by other terms, *mistress* appears to be moving toward obsolescence and is an unlikely candidate for rehabilitation.

Until a few years ago the post of "master" of a residential
college at Yale University was always filled by a male faculty
member. If the wife of a master also lived at the college and
shared his duties, she was called the "mistress" of the college. In
the early 1970s the university began to appoint women to the
post of master, and for a time there was confusion over the
designation. By the end of the decade, however, Yale seemed to
have taken a firm stand and was announcing the appointments
of female as well as male faculty members to the post of master.

The presence of *master* in many combinations like *masterful,
mastery, masterpiece,* and *mastermind* assures its continuance as a
useful sex-neutral term.

MIDWIFE

Another old word whose meaning has expanded is *midwife,* now
an accepted designation for a person of either sex trained to
assist at a birth. Although it was occasionally applied to male
practitioners in the eighteenth century, the word as well as the
practice lost status with the rise of modern medicine when midwifery was disparaged and even outlawed in most parts of the
United States. In the past two decades, however, the midwife
has made a dramatic comeback as a highly trained specialist.
Today nursing school programs in nurse-midwifery actively re-
cruit members of both sexes, and more than thirty-five hundred

certified nurse-midwives, including about two dozen men, are now practicing in this country.

Midwife initially meant "a woman" (the original meaning of *wife*) "with" *(mid)* another woman giving birth. Jokes have been made about sex-neutralizing the word to *midspouse,* but just as a person who practices midwifery does not have to be a wife in the modern sense of "married woman," so that person does not have to be a wife in the ancient sense of "woman." Like *master, midwife* has become a common-gender word. It has also acquired the additional meaning of "one that helps to produce or bring forth something." Shakespeare used it as a noun in *Richard II,*

> "thou art the midwife of my woe"

and it is sometimes used as a verb, as in

> "probably the first time in history that a bank midwived
> a successful biographical novel."

This figurative meaning of *midwife* is reinforced by another word, the adjective *maieutic,* which has to do with the Socratic method of eliciting and clarifying ideas and which comes from the Greek *maieuesthai,* "to act as midwife."

OLD WIVES' TALE

An "old wife," according to Webster's Third New International Dictionary, is "a prattling old woman: GOSSIP." That dictionary does not define *old wives' tale,* but others do. Its predecessor, Webster's Second, gives the meaning as "A tale, or bit of lore, or a notion, esp. a superstitious traditional notion, characteristic of old women," and the American Heritage Dictionary provides "A bit of superstitious folklore."

Like old men, old women can be garrulous and given to gossip and superstition. But they can also be sages, the possessors of great wisdom about human nature and human ills and their cures. It is this quality of wisdom that the phrase *old wives' tale,* as it has typically been used over some four hundred years, ignores. Compare, for example, a verse translated in the King James Version of the Bible as

"But refuse profane and old wives' fables . . ."

with the translation in the Revised Standard Version (1946), which is more faithful to the Greek original:

"Have nothing to do with godless and silly myths. . . ."

At a time when many women are insisting on a return to some of the humane techniques of midwifery which were lost when obstetrics became largely a male preserve, the following use, cited by the unabridged Random House Dictionary, is particularly ironic:

"Modern medicine has dispelled many old wives' tales about childbearing."

Interestingly, the Anglo-Saxon meaning of *wife* (i.e., "woman") is preserved in the phrase *old wives' tale*. Rather than abandon it, speakers and writers might well use *old wives' tale* to evoke the kind of valuable knowledge and insights women have traditionally passed along to one another from generation to generation.

Such a use is suggested by the following account. In 1775 the British physician William Withering heard about a folk remedy for the treatment of dropsy, an accumulation of fluid in the body associated with heart disease. "I was told that it had long been kept a secret by an old woman in Shropshire, who had sometimes made cures after the more regular practitioners had failed," Dr. Withering wrote. He persuaded the woman, identified only as a Mistress Hutton, to tell him her remedy, which, it turned out, was made from the leaves of the foxglove plant *Digitalis purpurea*. Using foxglove infusions on his own patients, Dr. Withering experimented with different dosages and eventually published his findings in 1785. Thus the discovery of digitalis was in reality the transfer of an old wives' tale into the body of information known to medical science.

PERSON

This useful word has been much reviled by people who think sexism in language is a trivial issue. Professor Jacques Barzun, writing about what he calls "the *person* binge of today," poses the question, "Who does not feel that in its most general sense, which asserts anonymity, the word is disagreeably hoity-toity: 'There is a person at the door'?" Lots of people, apparently, for although Professor Barzun rigs his example ("There's someone at the door" would be more natural), it is in the sense of "someone," "a human being who may be of either sex," that the term is most widely used today. As for precedent, nobody has complained that *person* is disagreeably hoity-toity in the United States Constitution where it is used repeatedly in reference to the President, Vice President, Senators, and Representatives, as well as to the citizenry: " . . . nor shall any state deprive any person of life, liberty, or property. . . ."

Unlike "generic" *man, person* clearly conveys common gender —which is why it is a frequent choice today to replace traditional *man* terms. A camping equipment store advertises

"Two-person Timberline Tents."

A form letter from the United States Small Business Administration describing government contract opportunities begins

"Dear Small Businessperson."

In his nationally syndicated column, William Safire refers to an argument that

"knocks down a strawperson."

A. M. Rosenthal of the *New York Times* writes of attempts to limit freedom of the press

" . . . fight like hell . . . against any attempts at press restrictions, particularly the ones that sound nice and reasonable—most newspersons are courageous enough to resist the hard-fisted ones."

And columnist Nicholas Von Hoffman comments on the discomfort experienced by public figures whose relatives write books or go on talk shows in order

"to cash in on their famous kinsperson."

Like a number of other religious bodies, the 5.3-million member Evangelical Lutheran Church in America has revised all its official documents to employ common-gender terms like *layperson* instead of *layman*.

One reason *person* is a special target of ridicule may be that it is frequently used unnecessarily and therefore awkwardly:

> "ABC College . . . recently released the names of
> students who have been placed on the Dean's List. One
> of the persons named to the list is . . ."

could be

> . . . One of those named to the list is. . . .

Similarly,

> "I married a person who believes that we have a
> partnership"

could be

> I married someone who believes we have a partnership

or, since the speaker was a woman,

> I married a man who believes we have a partnership.

Perhaps because of its association with efforts to achieve equality of the sexes, *person* is sometimes misunderstood (or misinterpreted) to mean "woman." When terms like *chairman* and *spokesman* are used for men while *chairperson, spokesperson*, etc., are reserved for women, the implication—conscious or otherwise—is that *woman* is a taboo word for which a euphemism must be substituted:

> "The Planning and Zoning Commission and the Board
> of Education last week elected new chairpersons. . . .
> James Doe, newly elected Planning and Zoning
> member . . . will serve as chairman. . . . Catherine Roe
> will serve as chairperson of the Board of
> Education. . . ."

This lopsided usage may also subtly derogate the woman referred to, as when a headline calling Golda Meir an "Elder Statesperson" appeared in a newspaper that at the time allowed neither *chairperson* nor *spokesperson* in its pages.

*　　　*　　　*

One pluralization of *person* is *people*. This is a common and natural usage, despite the frequently cited "rule" that *persons* is the correct form to use when referring to an exact or relatively small number of people. One would not say, for example,

> We're inviting a few persons over for supper

or

> Our church sheltered eight streetpersons during the storm.

Similarly, most compound words ending in *person* sound more natural when pluralized with *people:*

> Jewelry by three local craftspeople is displayed in the bank window.

> We have seventeen salespeople covering the north central states.

> According to their spokespeople, none of the candidates will campaign on Yom Kippur.

If *chairperson* survives intact, *chairpeople* may prove to be the natural and most acceptable plural.

The increased recognition being accorded *person* has led to the emergence of *personhood,* a word so new that few dictionaries define it. Now that *personhood* has become part of the lexicon, it is hard to see how English was able to get along without it. For example, neither *manhood* nor *womanhood* would have expressed the meaning Barbara Jordan intended when, supporting Congressional action to extend the ratification deadline for the Equal Rights Amendment, she asked,

> "Who am I to say we should short-circuit the time to seek personhood in society?"

Nor in the following statement could one substitute *womanhood* for *personhood:*

> "[Rape] is experienced by women as a total assault on their personhood. . . ."

SUFFRAGIST, SUFFRAGETTE

A resolution supporting suffrage for women was first presented to the British Parliament in 1851, but for more than half a century neither the government nor the press paid much attention to the cause, its leaders, or the growing numbers of women and men in British suffrage societies. In 1903 Emmeline Pankhurst and her daughters, Christabel and Sylvia, formed the Women's Social and Political Union (WSPU) with the aim of publicizing their demand for enfranchisement by heckling politicians at meetings and by demonstrations and acts of civil disobedience.

The technique worked. The activities of the militant suffragists were soon being reported regularly by British newspapers, often—to be sure—with scorn or amused condescension, but the WSPU leaders believed that any attention was better than none. One paper referred to the militants as "martyrettes," and in 1906 the *Daily Mail* coined the term *suffragette,* which the WSPU immediately adopted, hardening the "g." As Christabel Pankhurst later wrote, "Just 'want the vote' was the notion conveyed by the older appellation [but] as a famous anecdote had it, 'the Suffragettes, they mean to get it.' "

Not all militant British suffragists were enthusiastic about the name. A comment by the historian Trevor Lloyd is revealing: "[T]he supporters of the Suffrage Societies were known as Suffragists, so *it was natural* to call their more violent allies in the WSPU 'Suffragettes.' " (Italics added.) Since the *-ette* ending in English also signals either small size or imitation, attaching it to the "more violent allies" could only be considered "natural" as an uneasy effort to discount them. Lloyd (writing in 1971) adds that "by now almost everyone who supported votes for women in the days before the First World War is liable to be called a suffragette. But at the time the suffragettes were a very special group—they did not always like the nickname, and sometimes called themselves 'militants'—with a special approach to politics."

In the United States, opponents of women's suffrage, including a powerful antisuffrage press, were quick to apply the derisive *suffragette* to American women seeking the vote. The great majority of those who worked in the movement from 1848 to 1920, however—including Elizabeth Cady Stanton, Lucretia Mott, Susan B. Anthony, Lucy Stone, Ida B. Wells, Anna Howard Shaw, Mary Church Terrell, Carrie Chapman Catt, and Alice Paul—called themselves "suffragists." To call them "suffragettes" is both historically inaccurate and trivializing.

"SURROGACY"

The vocabulary growing up around high-tech methods of human reproduction provides an instructive example of how terminology can be used to alter human values. The new vocabulary falls roughly into two categories: terms like "miracle baby," "biomom," "borrowed womb," and "fetal baby-sitter" sound friendly and reassuring, lulling us into complacency; more technical terms like "noncoital collaborative reproduction," "donated embryo transfer," and "gestational mother" sound detached and unemotional, all the while obscuring the fact that what we are really talking about are the most intimate and personal aspects of people's lives.

"Surrogate mother" may evoke an image of generosity and prestige, a new and honored role made possible by miracles of science. But remembering Hagar, who in another age performed an accepted and somewhat similar service for the childless Abraham and Sarah, may be closer to the mark: women recruited to gestate and bear children for others rarely attain the levels of wealth or professional standing that are the real measures of prestige in most societies. And when, as today, such techniques as gamete banking and embryo implantation are added, women predisposed by economic necessity to sell their reproductive services become even more at risk.

It is in this area that the language of "surrogacy" is most revealing. Expressions like "incubator mother," "rented womb," "alternative reproduction vehicle," and "baby factory" are more appropriately used of machines than of human beings. They are mechanistic, and they suggest monetary as well as physical exploitation not only of individuals but also of young, impoverished women as a class.

The new terminology is also often used in a way that perpetuates the ancient myth that women's contribution to procreation is less valuable than men's. This was clear in the Baby M case, for example, when references to the baby's "father" or "natural father" or "biological father" were routinely juxtaposed with references to her "surrogate mother"—although the woman so identified is every bit as much the baby's mother as the provider of sperm is her father.

Whether on a conscious level or a subliminal one, this new language can move our attitudes about conception and birth out of the realm of the personal, where human values are paramount, into the realm of economic and political power. It can help to prepare us for a world in which the "production" of babies for profit or geopolitical advantage has become an acceptable idea, hiding the possibility of exploitation on a grand scale. But if the language of surrogacy can be negatively manipulative, it can also serve a positive function, for it calls attention to trends that, if allowed to go unchallenged, will become more and more difficult to reverse.

TOMBOY

The implication of the word *tomboy* is that an active, inquisitive, energetic girl acts like a boy, not a girl. In other words, she is abnormal for one of her sex.

Seldom is the socialization of children reflected more directly in language than in this term, although the word *sissy* comes close, especially when applied to a boy. Perhaps the chief difference in the effect of the two words is that *sissy*, which comes from *sister* (just as *buddy* comes from *brother*), is an overt insult whereas *tomboy* purports to be a compliment. In the first instance the child's answer can be clear and self-enhancing: "I'm *not* a sissy!" In the second, neither denial nor assent is appropriate.

Although English lacks sex-specific words to describe the kind of girl who is labeled a "tomboy," it does have an abundance of sex-neutral terms to choose from. Words like *strong, vigorous, direct, adventurous, spirited, self-confident, competitive,* and *physically courageous* can serve the same purpose without confusing the child's self-perception and sense of sexual identity.

WOMEN'S LIBERATION

People who use the term *women's lib* probably would not dream of saying "black lib" or "lib for Native Americans," and they may not realize what this offhand treatment of a serious subject reveals about their attitudes. Abbreviations like *black lib, women's lib,* and *fem lib* are apt to be the hallmark of either hostile or shallow thinking.

The social movement to achieve rights and opportunities for women equal to those of men, whether one agrees with it or not, is a historic fact. When its goals are achieved, the terms *feminism, women's movement,* and *women's liberation* will be of historic interest only.

Perhaps the most positive effect of changing our linguistic practice will be to destroy the pernicious belief that we have to be controlled and oppressed by our language. Once over that hurdle, we can start learning to speak out with confidence and to use the resources of language and metalanguage, so often denied us or used against us, in the continuing struggle against patriarchy.

—Deborah Cameron, *Feminism and Linguistic Theory*

[T]he power to determine linguistic usage has in the past been reserved largely to men; by participating in the reform of sexist usage, women have begun to appropriate some of the power to themselves. They have begun to add to our language terms which describe women's experience from women's own point of view. . . . Language is the common heritage of humans; all humans must share in shaping and using it.

—Francine Frank and Frank Anshen
Language and the Sexes

A Brief Thesaurus

An asterisk (*) indicates that the word or phrase is discussed in the text and listed in the Index.

Want to Avoid?	**Try . . .**
Actress*	Actor
Adventuress	Adventurer
Alumnae,* alumni*	Graduates, alums, alumnae/i
Ambassadress	Ambassador
Ancestress	Ancestor, foremother
Anchorman	Anchor
Authoress	Author
Aviatrix	Aviator

Want to Avoid?	**Try . . .**
Baseman	Base player
Bellboy, bellman	Bellhop
Benefactress	Benefactor
Brakeman (bobsled)	Brake operator
Brakeman (train)	Conductor's assistant
Busboy, busgirl	Waiter's helper, waiter's (*or* serving) assistant
Businessmen	Business people
Career girl*	Business woman
Cavemen	Cave dwellers, cave people
Chairman,* chairwoman*	Chair, head, presider, presiding officer, convener, leader, moderator, coordinator
Clergymen	Clergy, clerics, members of the clergy
Coed* (noun)	Student
Comedienne	Comedian
Concertmistress	Concertmaster
Confidence man	Swindler
Congressmen*	Representatives, Congressional representatives, members of Congress, Congress people
Copy boy, copy girl	Copy clerk, runner
Craftsmen*	Craftspeople, artisans, craft workers, crafters
Creatrix	Creator, Maker
Deliveryman	Deliverer, delivery clerk, courier
Directress	Director, administrator, conductor

Doorman	Doorkeeper, doorkeep
Draftsman	Drafter
Drum majorette	Drum major, baton twirler
Enchantress	Enchanter, sorcerer, magician, fascinating woman
Englishman, Englishwoman	Englander, Briton
Equestrienne	Equestrian, rider, horseback rider
Executrix	Executor
Farmerette,* farmeress*	Farmer
Fireman	Fire fighter, stoker (ships and trains)
Fisherman*	Fisher, angler
Flagman	Flagger
Forefathers*	Ancestors, forebears, foremothers and forefathers
Forelady,* foreman*	Supervisor, boss, leader, head juror
Frenchmen	The French
Freshmen	First-year students, yearlings
Gentleman's agreement	Unwritten agreement, agreement based on trust
Girl Friday, man Friday	Aide, key aide, assistant, helper
Goddess*	God
Handyman	Fixer, jack-of-all-trades
Heiress	Heir, inheritor

Want to Avoid?	Try . . .
Heroine*	Hero
Horseman, horsewoman	Rider, equestrian
Hostess*	Host
Housewife,* househusband	Homemaker
Huntress	Hunter
Husbandman	Farmer, husbander
Inspectress	Inspector
Instructress	Instructor, teacher
Kinsmen	Kin, kinfolk, relatives
Laundress	Launderer, laundry worker
Laymen*	Lay people, laity
Mailman	Mail carrier, letter carrier, postal worker
Man,* mankind* (meaning the human species)	The human species, *Homo sapiens,* humans, humanity, humankind, the human family, human beings, human societies, people, we, us
Man* (meaning person)	Person, one, individual, you, I
Man* (as verb)	Operate, work, staff, serve at (*or* on *or* in)
Manageress	Manager
Man-hours*	Work-hours, labor time
Man-made*	Handmade, hand-built, human-made, synthetic, manufactured, fabricated, machine-

	made, constructed, simulated
Man of letters*	Literary person, writer, author, pundit
Man of the Year	Newsmaker of the Year
Manpower*	Personnel, staff, human resources, labor, people power, muscle power
Man-to-man	One-to-one, one-on-one, person-to-person
Matron	Married woman, supervisor, prison guard
Mediatress, mediatrix	Mediator
Meter maid	Meter attendant, meter tender, meter reader
Middleman	Contact, go-between, intermediary, agent
Murderess	Murderer
Newsman*	Newsperson, reporter, journalist
Number one man	Head, chief, number one
Number two man	Second in command, chief aide
Office boy, office girl	Office helper, office assistant, clerk
One man, one vote	One person, one vote
One-man show	One-person show, solo show, one-artist show
One-upsmanship	The art of one-upping
Patroness	Patron, benefactor, sponsor, mentor
Pitchman	Hawker, promoter
Poetess	Poet

Want to Avoid?	**Try . . .**
Policeman, policewoman	Police officer
Postmistress	Postmaster
Priestess	Priest
Procuress	Procurer, pander
Prophetess	Prophet
Proprietress	Proprietor, owner, owner-manager
Repairman	Repairer
Rewriteman	Rewriter
Right-hand man	Chief assistant, lieutenant
Salesman,* saleswoman,* saleslady, salesgirl	Salesclerk, salesperson, sales agent, sales representative (*or* rep)
Scotsman	Scot, Scotlander
Sculptress	Sculptor
Seaman	Sailor, mariner, seafarer
Seamstress	Tailor, needleworker
Seductress	Seducer
Seeress	Prophet, seer, clairvoyant
Shepherdess	Shepherd, pastor
Signalman	Signal operator, signaler
Songstress	Singer
Sorceress	Sorcerer, enchanter
Spaceman	Astronaut, spacefarer, space traveler
Spokesman,* spokeswoman*	Spokesperson, representative
Sportsmanlike	Sporting
Sportsmanship*	Fair play, fairness
Starlet	Young star, star in the making
State policeman	State trooper, trooper

Statesmanlike	Diplomatic
Stewardess*	Steward (ship, union shop), flight attendant (aircraft)
Straw man	Straw, straw person
Suffragette*	Suffragist
Surrogate mother	Biological (or natural) mother, gestational mother
Switchman	Switch operator
Temptress	Tempter, enticer
Testatrix	Testator
Tragedienne	Tragedian, actor who plays tragic roles
Traitoress, traitress	Traitor, betrayer
Trashman	Trash collector
Usherette	Usher
Villainess	Villain, scoundrel
Waitress*	Waiter, server
Wardress	Warden, prison warden, warder, guardian, keeper
Watchman*	Watch, guard
Weatherman,* weather girl*	Weather reporter, weather caster, forecaster, meteorologist
Workman	Worker
Workmanlike	Efficient, skillful

More extensive listings of words and phrases with nonsexist alternatives are available in:

Mary Ellen S. Capek, editor, *A Women's Thesaurus: An Index of*

Language Used to Describe and Locate Information By and About Women, a project of the National Council for Research on Women and the Business and Professional Women's Foundation, New York, Harper & Row, 1988.

Rosalie Maggio, *The Nonsexist Word Finder: A Dictionary of Gender-Free Usage,* Phoenix, The Oryx Press, 1987.

Maxims Maximized

Folk wisdom contained in proverbs is often phrased in—or translated into—*he/man* terms. Such sayings can be adapted by anyone who wants to use them with reference to everyone. For example:

One man's meat is another man's poison. 　　　　—Lucretius	What is food to one is poison to another. 　　　　—Jim Hartz
Give a man a fish and he'll eat for a day. Teach him to fish and he'll eat forever.	Give someone a fish and they'll eat for a day. Teach them to fish and they'll eat forever.
To each his own.	To each one's own.
He who hesitates is lost.	One who hesitates is lost.
Time and tide wait for no man.	Time and tide wait for no one.
He who has a thousand friends has not a friend to spare.	Those who have a thousand friends have not a friend to spare.
Ours is a government of laws and not of men.	Ours is a government of laws and not of people.
He who laughs last laughs best.	The last laugh is the best.

Inclusive Language Resources for Religious Worship

An Inclusive Language Lectionary. Scripture readings in three volumes for voluntary use in public worship, prepared under the aegis of the National Council of Churches of Christ in the USA and published by John Knox Press, Atlanta; the Pilgrim Press, New York; and the Westminster Press, Philadelphia, 1984–1986.

Language and the Church, Barbara A. Withers, editor. A collection of articles and workshop designs on Biblical authority and nonsexist interpretation published by the National Council of Churches of Christ in the USA.

Information and order forms for the two publications above are available from the Division of Education and Ministry, NCCC, 475 Riverside Drive, Room 704, New York, N.Y. 10115–0050.

Out of the House of Bondage, 1982 supplement to the *New Union Haggadah,* prepared by the Task Force on Equality of Women in Judaism of the New York Federation of Reform Synagogues.

Shabbat Evening Service, adapted from *Gates of Prayer* by the Task Force on Equality of Women in Judaism.

The American Spirit: An Interreligious Thanksgiving Service, produced by the Department of Interreligious Affairs, Union of American Hebrew Congregations (with guidelines for Jews and Christians in joint worship).

164

Information and order forms for the above are available from the Commission on Social Action/Interreligious Affairs, Union of American Hebrew Congregations, 838 Fifth Avenue, New York, N.Y. 10021.

The Women's Ordination Conference Book of Liturgies, Elaine Marie Crumby Clipson, Fidelis McDonough, and Eileen Hanrahan Queener, editors, 1987. Available from Women's Ordination Conference, P.O. Box 2693, Fairfax, Va. 22031.

Women-Church: Theology and Practice of Feminist Liturgical Communities, Rosemary Radford Ruether, San Francisco, Harper & Row, 1985.

Jewish and Female: Choices and Changes in Our Lives Today, Susan Weidman Schneider, New York, Simon and Schuster, 1984.

Miriam's Well: Rituals for Jewish Women Around the Year, Penina V. Adelman, Biblio Press, 1986. Available from Biblio Press, P.O. Box 22, Fresh Meadows, N.Y. 11365.

Women and Worship: A Guide to Non-Sexist Hymns, Prayers, and Liturgies, rev. ed., Sharon and Thomas Neufer Emswiler, New York, Harper & Row, 1984.

The Word for Us: The Gospels of John and Mark, Epistles to the Romans and the Galatians, Restated in Inclusive Language, Joann Haugerud, Seattle, Coalition on Women and Religion, 1977. Available from Coalition on Women and Religion, 4759 15th Avenue, Northeast, Seattle, Wash. 98105.

Book of Worship of the United Church of Christ, 1987. Available from UCC Church Leadership Resources, 1400 North 7th Street, St. Louis, Mo. 63106.

A Seder for the Sisters of Sarah, Diann Neu. A dinner liturgy for Jewish and Christian women. Available from Women's Alliance for Theology, Ethics and Ritual—WATER, 8035 13th Street, Suite 3, Silver Spring, Md. 20910.

Psalms Anew, Nancy Schreck and Maureen Leach, St. Mary's Press, Terrace Heights, Winona, Minn. 55987.

Lectionary for the Christian People. Scripture readings for use by Lutherans, Episcopalians, and Roman Catholics. New York, Pueblo Publishing Company, 1986, in cooperation with Fortress Press.

Guide to Inclusive Hymn/Song Resources. One-page annotated bibliography developed by the General Commission on the Status and Role of Women in the United Methodist Church. Send self-addressed, stamped envelope to GCSRW, 1200 Davis Street, Evanston, Ill. 60201.

Reference Notes

In addition to the specific references cited in these notes, we found the following papers of particular interest and would like to acknowledge their contributions to our thinking:

Phyllis R. Randall, "Sexist Language and Speech Communication Texts: Another Case of Benign Neglect," *Communication Education,* April 1985, Vol. 34, pp. 128–134.

Julia Penelope, "Two Essays on Language and Change," *College English,* December 1982, Vol. 44, No. 8, pp. 840–854.

Nancy M. Henley, "This New Species That Seeks a New Language: On Sexism in Language and Language Change," paper presented at the Conference on Language and Gender, University of California at Santa Cruz, May 4, 1979.

Patricia C. Nichols, "Planning for Language Change," paper presented at the Modern Language Association of America Forum on Women and Language, New York, December 27–30, 1978.

Maija S. Blaubergs, "Sociolinguistic Change Towards Nonsexist Language: An Overview and Analysis of Misunderstandings and Misapplications," paper presented at the Ninth World Congress of Sociology, Uppsala, Sweden, August 1978.

INTRODUCTION

Page 2 The study of three dictionaries of new words was conducted by Garland Cannon and Susan Roberson, Department of English, Texas A&M University, and reported by them in "Sexism in Present-Day English: Is It Diminishing?" *Word,* the journal of the International Linguistic Association, April 1985, Vol. 36, No. 1, pp. 23–35. *Women and Language,* edited by Cheris Kramarae and Paula A. Treichler, is an interdisciplinary research periodical published at the University of Illinois in Urbana-Champaign.

Pages 6–7 The Chisholm quotation is from Shirley Chisholm, "The 51% Minority," in *The American Sisterhood: Writings of the Feminist Movement from Colonial Times to the Present,* Wendy Martin, editor, New York, Harper & Row, 1972.

CHAPTER 1   *MAN* AS A FALSE GENERIC

Page 13 Among studies which report and discuss evidence indicating that the so-called generics *man* and *men* (and compounds incorporating them) are not generally understood to include females are the following:

Nancy L. Murdock and Donelson R. Forsyth, "Is Gender-Biased Language Sexist? A Perceptual Approach," in *Psychology of Women Quarterly,* March 1985, Vol. 9, No. 1, pp. 39–49.

Mykol C. Hamilton and Nancy M. Henley, "Detrimental Consequences of Generic Masculine Usage," paper presented at the meeting of the Western Psychological Association, Sacramento, Calif., April 1982.

Johanna S. DeStefano, Mary W. Kuhner, and Harold B. Pepinsky, "An Investigation of Referents of Selected Sex-Indefinite Terms in English," paper presented at the Ninth World Congress of Sociology, Uppsala, Sweden, August 1978.

LaVisa Cam Wilson, "Teachers' Inclusion of Males and Females in Generic Nouns," *Research in the Teaching of English,* May 1978, Vol. 12, No. 2, pp. 155–161.

Ozella M. Y. Eberhart, "Elementary Students' Understanding of Certain Masculine and Neutral Generic Nouns," doctoral dissertation, Kansas State University, 1976, *Dissertation Abstracts,* 1976, Vol. 37, pp. 4113A–4114A. (University Microfilms No. 76–29,993)

Linda Harrison, "Cro-Magnon Woman—In Eclipse," *The Science Teacher,* April 1975, pp. 8–11.

Linda Harrison and Richard Passero, "Sexism in the Language

of Elementary School Textbooks," *Science and Children*, January 1975, Vol. 12, pp. 22–25.

Joseph W. Schneider and Sally L. Hacker, "Sex Role Imagery and the Use of the Generic 'Man' in Introductory Texts: A Case in the Sociology of Sociology," *The American Sociologist*, February 1973, Vol. 8, No. 1, pp. 12–18. See also Sally L. Hacker, "Man and Humanism: An Essay on Language, Gender and Power," *Humanity & Society*, November 1978, Vol. 2, No. 4, pp. 273–282.

For an analysis of the cognitive exclusion of women in common "generic" uses of *man*, see Julia P. Stanley, "Gender-Marking in American English: Usage and Reference," in Alleen Pace Nilsen, Haig Bosmajian, H. Lee Gershuny, and Julia P. Stanley, *Sexism and Language*, Urbana, Ill., National Council of Teachers of English, 1977.

An interesting discussion of the "reasonable man" doctrine in law and its nonapplicability to women is provided by Ronald K. L. Collins in "Language, History and the Legal Process: A Profile of the 'Reasonable Man,' " *Rutgers-Camden Law Journal*, Winter 1977, Vol. 8, No. 2, pp. 311–323.

Page 35 "Were our State a pure democracy . . ." is from a letter to Samuel Kerchval dated September 5, 1816, reprinted in *The Works of Thomas Jefferson*, Paul Leicester Ford, editor, New York, G. P. Putnam's Sons, 1905, Federal Edition, Vol. 12, pp. 15–16.

Page 36 The effect of sex-labeled job titles on students' perceptions of career options was studied by Sandra and Daryl Bem and reported in their article "Does Sex-Biased Job Advertising 'Aid and Abet' Sex Discrimination?" *Journal of Applied Social Psychology*, January–March 1973, Vol. 3, No. 1, pp. 6–18. A similar study was conducted by N. Shepelak, D. Ogden, and D. Tobin at Indiana University. A brief description of the results appears in Norma J. Shepelak, "Neanderthal Person Revisited," *The American Sociologist*, May 1976, Vol. 11, No. 2, pp. 90–92.

CHAPTER 2   THE PRONOUN PROBLEM

Page 44 The historical background on "generic" *he* is drawn primarily from two sources: Ann Bodine, "Androcentrism and

Prescriptive Grammar: Singular 'They,' Sex-Indefinite 'He,' and 'He or She,' " *Language in Society,* August 1975, Vol. 4, No. 2, pp. 129–145; and Julia P. Stanley, "Sexist Grammar," *College English,* March 1978, Vol. 39, No. 7, pp. 800–811.

Page 45 Reports of studies confirming the failure of "generic" *he* to represent both sexes adequately include the following:

Mykol C. Hamilton, "Effects of the Masculine 'Generic' on Imagery and Perception," paper presented at the annual meeting of the American Psychological Association, Los Angeles, Calif., August 1985, based on the author's doctoral dissertation, *Dissertation Abstracts International,* 1985, Vol. 46, p. 1381B. (University Microfilms No. 85–13,117)

Janet Shibley Hyde, "Children's Understanding of Sexist Language," *Developmental Psychology,* 1984, Vol. 20, No. 4, pp. 697–706.

Donald G. MacKay, "Prescriptive Grammar and the Pronoun Problem," in Barrie Thorne, Cheris Kramarae, and Nancy Henley, editors, *Language, Gender and Society,* Rowley, Mass., Newbury House, 1983, pp. 38–53.

Wendy Martyna, "Beyond the He/Man Approach: The Case for Nonsexist Language," in Thorne, Kramarae, and Henley, *Language, Gender and Society,* cited above, pp. 25–37.

Jeanette Silveira, "Generic Masculine Words and Thinking," *Women's Studies International Quarterly,* 1980, Vol. 3, Nos. 2 and 3.

Janice Moulton, George M. Robinson, and Cherin Elias, "Sex Bias in Language Use: 'Neutral' Pronouns That Aren't," *American Psychologist,* November 1978, Vol. 33, No. 11, pp. 1032–1036.

DeStefano, Kuhner, and Pepinsky, "An Investigation of Referents of Selected Sex-Indefinite Terms in English," cited above.

Barbara Bate, "Nonsexist Language Use in Transition," *Journal of Communication,* Winter 1978, Vol. 28, No. 1, pp. 139–149.

Virginia Kidd, "A Study of the Images Produced Through the Use of the Male Pronoun as the Generic," *Moments in Contemporary Rhetoric and Communication,* 1971, Vol. 1, No. 2, pp. 25–30.

Pages 57–58 A review of recently proposed common-gender pronouns and examples of their use in published materials appears in Casey Miller and Kate Swift, *Words and Women*, Garden City, N.Y., Anchor Press/Doubleday, 1977, pp. 116–118. For a detailed historical perspective on proposed common-gender pronouns, see Dennis E. Baron, "The Epicene Pronoun: The Word that Failed," *American Speech*, Summer 1981, Vol. 56, pp. 83–97.

Experiments testing the effectiveness of various proposed sex-inclusive pronouns were conducted by Donald G. MacKay and his colleagues in the Department of Psychology, University of California at Los Angeles.

CHAPTER 3 GENERALIZATIONS

Page 63 The information on farmers in developing countries is from Kristin Helmore, "The Neglected Resource: Women in the Developing World," *The Christian Science Monitor*, December 17, 18, 19, 20, and 23, 1985; and John J. Gilligan, "Women and Their Importance to the Third World," *The Washington Post*, June 24, 1978.

Page 76 The Poole quotation appears in Bodine, "Androcentrism in Prescriptive Grammar," cited above. The Murray quotation appears in Stanley, "Sexist Grammar," also cited above.

CHAPTER 4 SEEING WOMEN AND GIRLS AS PEOPLE

Page 84 A discerning discussion of the terms that mental health professionals use in referring to female patients is provided by Harriet E. Lerner, "Girls, Ladies, or Women? The Unconscious Dynamics of Language Choice," *Comprehensive Psychiatry*, March/April 1976, Vol. 17, No. 2, pp. 295–299. The psycholinguist Ethel Strainchamps postulates that one reason people avoid *woman* is because it phonetically symbolizes small size and low status. Strainchamps's discoveries about the gender system of English, in which sounds reflect consensus not only on size and shape but on status and sex associations, are discussed in Miller and Swift, *Words and Women*, cited above, p. 162.

Page 92 The study of the qualities people consider typical of a "girl," a "lady," and a "woman" was conducted by William J. McCarthy and his colleagues in the Department of Psychology, University of California at Los Angeles, and was presented under the title "Social Influences on What to Call Her: 'Woman,' 'Girl,' or 'Lady'" at the annual meeting of the American Psychological Association in Los Angeles, August 1985.

Page 93 We wish to thank Marjorie Vogel of Pittsburgh, Pennsylvania, for sharing with us her insights on the language used to describe the work women and men do at home.

Page 95 The eight-part series of articles entitled "Women at Work" appeared in the *Wall Street Journal* between August 28 and September 22, 1978.

CHAPTER 5   PARALLEL TREATMENT

Page 115 Mary Ritchie Key discusses categories in her book *Male/Female Language,* Metuchen, N.J., The Scarecrow Press, 1975, pp. 82–83.

Page 117 The Wilson quotation appears in Bodine, "Androcentrism in Prescriptive Grammar," cited above.

Page 124 The inscription on a gravestone in the Duck River Cemetery in Old Lyme, Connecticut, reads:
        "Ms Ruth Noyes   September 14, 1690   Age 30"
Next to Ruth Noyes' stone is that of her husband, Moses Noyes.

Page 125 We wish to thank Jane Mollman, who also likes to be referred to as Mrs. J. Peter Mollman, for allowing us to use her poem "In typing *Ms.* for *Mrs.*"

CHAPTER 6   A FEW MORE WORDS

Page 130 The inclusion of both the masculine- and feminine-gender forms of personal nouns and pronouns in the Latin of Roman law is discussed, with examples, by Otto Jespersen in *Language: Its Nature, Development and Origin,* New York, Henry Holt and Company, 1922, pp. 347–348.

Pages 132–133 Discussion of the title *Esq.* appeared in the *Denver*

Post, March 4, 1976, p. 36. Alette Hill's comments on the subject are from personal correspondence.

Page 139   The study of how college students interpret the word *feminist* was conducted by Cynthia Berryman-Fink, University of Cincinnati, and Kathleen S. Verderber, Northern Kentucky University, and reported in "Attributions of the Term *Feminist*: A Factor Analytic Development of a Measuring Instrument," *Psychology of Women Quarterly,* March 1985, Vol. 9, No. 1, pp. 51–63.

Page 146   The account of the discovery of digitalis, including the Withering quotation, is from Margaret B. Kreig, *Green Medicine: The Search for Plants That Heal,* Chicago, Rand McNally & Company, 1964, pp. 207–214.

Page 150   The Pankhurst quotation is from Christabel Pankhurst, *Unshackled: The Story of How We Won the Vote,* edited by the Rt. Hon. Lord Pethick-Lawrence of Peasdale, London, Hutchison, 1959, pp. 62–63. The Lloyd quotation is from Trevor Lloyd, *Suffragettes International: The World-Wide Campaign for Women's Rights,* New York, American Heritage Press, and London, Macdonald Unit 75, 1971, p. 49.

The quotations that precede chapter openings are from the following publications:

Page 1   Horace, *Art of Poetry,* quoted in Karl W. Dykema, "Grammar," Encyclopaedia Britannica, Chicago, William Benton, Publisher, 1971, Vol. 10, p. 666; William Safire, "On Language," *The New York Times Magazine,* July 3, 1983, pp. 6–7.

Page 11   Elaine Morgan, *The Descent of Woman,* New York, Stein and Day, 1972, p. 3.

Page 43   Dale Spender, *Man Made Language,* Routledge & Kegan Paul, 1980, pp. 2–3; Deborah Cameron, *Feminism and Linguistic Theory,* New York, St. Martin's Press, 1985, p. 73.

Page 59   Philip M. Smith, *Language, the Sexes and Society,* New York, Basil Blackwell, 1985, p. 31.

Page 80   Smith, *Language, the Sexes and Society,* cited above, p. 19.

Page 101   Douglas R. Hofstadter, *Metamagical Themas: Questing for the Essence of Mind and Pattern,* New York, Basic Books, 1985, p. 158.

Page 129   Spender, *Man Made Language,* cited above, p. 162; Cheris Kramarae, *Women and Men Speaking: Framework for Analysis,* Rowley, Mass., Newbury House, 1981, p. 114.

Page 155   Cameron, *Feminism and Linguistic Theory,* cited above, p. 173; Francine Frank and Frank Anshen, *Language and the Sexes,* Albany, N.Y., State University of New York Press, 1983, p. 93.

Index

175